# Elections and Conflict Management in Africa

# Elections and Conflict Management in Africa

**TIMOTHY D. SISK** and **ANDREW REYNOLDS, Editors**

**UNITED STATES INSTITUTE OF PEACE PRESS**
Washington, D.C.

United States Institute of Peace
1550 M Street NW, Suite 700
Washington, DC 20005-1708

First published 1998
Second printing 1999
Printed in the United States of America

The paper used in this publication meets the minimum requirements of American National Standard for Information Sciences—Permanence of Paper for Printed Library Materials, ANSI Z39.48-1984.

**Library of Congress Cataloging-in-Publication Data**
Elections and conflict management in Africa / Timothy D. Sisk and
  Andrew Reynolds, editors.
     p. cm.
  Includes bibliographical references and index.
  ISBN 1-878379-79-8 (pbk.)
  1. Elections—Africa. 2. Representative government and representa-
tion—Africa. 3. Conflict management—Africa. 4. Africa—Ethnic
relations—Political aspects. I. Sisk, Timothy D., 1960–. II. Reynolds,
Andrew, 1967–.
JQ1879.A5E43 1998
324.96—dc21                                                    98-16504
                                                                  CIP

*To Victoria and Madeline*

# CONTENTS

# ■ Introduction

# DEMOCRATIZATION, ELECTIONS, AND CONFLICT MANAGEMENT IN AFRICA
## Exploring the Nexus

In the 1990s, nearly all of Africa's fifty-four states have undergone dramatic political changes. Whether through transitions from war to negotiated peace agreements, through guided reforms to multiparty politics, or through battlefield victories that swept rebel movements into power, the stereotypical African one-party state—a common pattern of politics since rapid decolonization and independence began in the early 1960s—is a relic of the past. Africa has seen scores of new governments come to power seeking to inaugurate a new era that displaces the paradigmatic one-party or military-led "patrimonial" states that held sway over the continent for thirty years. In sum, a second independence has dawned.

Africa's second independence has brought with it a spate of elections, more than twenty between 1992 and 1994. In countries previously racked by armed conflict, elections often occurred as the capstone of war termination efforts. The international community, often personified as a UN peacekeeping operation or an election verification mission, advocated an election as *the* principal terminal point of efforts to replace civil wars with sustainable, peaceful politics. Angola, Eritrea, Ethiopia, Liberia, Namibia, Mozambique, Sierra Leone, South Africa, and Uganda, for example, held internationally monitored elections in the wake of years of civil conflict.

Elections have also served as the high points of political reforms that ushered in multiparty democracy. Pressures for democratization in Africa's one-party or military-ruled states mounted. External donors set good governance as a condition of their aid, and popular demands for political liberalization and accountability intensified. Ghana, Kenya, Malawi, and Zambia, for example, held high-profile elections that ushered in a new era of multiparty politics.

The track record of elections in Africa, however, remains quite mixed. Many Africans and external observers alike remain skeptical about the appropriateness and the ultimate utility of elections as an instrument of political change. Some decry the multiparty elections that have been held since the turn of the decade as the consequence of pressures by Western donors that usually fail to introduce democracy and often exacerbate tensions in Africa's invariably multiethnic, often polarized, societies. Disillusionment with elections is widespread, both among some African elites and in donor states.

There is good reason to be skeptical about the value of elections in societies such as those found in Africa. Elections *can* exacerbate social tensions by further polarizing highly conflictual societies. This is true particularly when incumbent regimes manipulate election rules to their own advantage.[1] One of the most poignant examples of the failure of elections to promote democracy or manage conflict in Africa is the 1994 election in Africa's most populous state, Nigeria. Rather than accepting the apparent will of the people, Nigeria's military intervened and halted the democratization process; the country remains tenuously poised between authoritarian stagnation and widespread civil unrest. In Angola in 1992, the peace process failed at the election moment when the losing party (UNITA, the National Union for the Total Independence of Angola) returned to the battlefield rather than accepting a likely defeat for its presidential candidate, Jonas Savimbi. The war raged for another two years before a peace settlement was eventually struck, a settlement that implicitly defers new elections for the foreseeable future.

Despite these examples of failed elections, others see the elections in Africa as the only way to create truly legitimate governments that protect human rights, govern accountably, and genuinely represent the people. Although imperfect in many respects, elections—even in Africa's predominantly rural, semiliterate, and deeply divided multiethnic societies—are the only vehicle through which democracy and long-lasting, peaceful politics can begin to take root. This view is common among grassroots democratizers and some scholars in the international community, and those who adopt it assert that efforts should focus on improving elections in Africa rather than dwelling on their shortcomings.

Some democratization experiments in the 1990s were successful, in that legitimate government has been reconstituted and the stage set for a longer term evolution to full democracy and its consolidation. In Benin, Eritrea, Madagascar, Mali, Mozambique, Namibia, South Africa, and Uganda, elections have been more or less successful vehicles for establishing fledgling democracies or at least starting down that road. Conflicts that formerly had been waged in the battlefield in these societies are increasingly arbitrated through the ballot box and on the floor of parliament.

The fact that elections can turn a society toward greater conflict or greater cooperation underscores the fact that processes of democratization and conflict management are inherently linked. Democratization does not inexorably lead to better conflict management, as might be expected, and the end of armed conflict does not lead inexorably to a new democracy, as would be hoped.

To investigate the nexus between elections and conflict management in Africa, the United States Institute of Peace held a symposium in June 1995 on these interrelated themes. The symposium brought academic experts on democracy and electoral processes together with representatives of international organizations, the U.S. government, and nongovernmental organizations (NGOs) active in Africa. This volume includes revised and updated versions of some of the papers presented at that symposium, augmented by a chapter written by the editors that provides an analytical prism through which to assess the many different roles of elections in democratization and conflict resolution. The concluding chapter draws upon the discussion at the conference to derive some generalized findings and policy recommendations.

This volume focuses on the role of electoral systems—the rules and procedures under which votes are translated into seats in parliament or the selection of executives—as a critical variable in determining whether elections can simultaneously serve the purposes of democratization and conflict management. Electoral systems are critically important for promoting democratization and conflict management because they are highly manipulable instruments of "constitutional engineering." Constitutions, including electoral law, establish the rules for the political game. The premise of constitutional engineering is that the rules can be established to provide structural incentives for moderate, conflict-mitigating behavior on the part of politicians. The rules under which elections are held have a strong bearing on whether they will have conflict-exacerbating or conflict-mitigating effects.

Thus, part I of this book addresses the following questions:

- How are elections related to democratization and conflict management processes?
- What are electoral systems, and what effects do they have on conflict management?
- How are elections related to other mechanisms that manage conflict in mature democracies, such as the full array of political institutions?
- Can power sharing and constitutional engineering help manage conflict, particularly ethnic conflict, in Africa?

The editors take the view that elections—if sequenced, structured, and conducted properly—are appropriate instruments of conflict management through democratization. The approach adopted by the editors, more fully developed in chapter 1, places an analytical premium on the role of institutional design and constitutional engineering in efforts to simultaneously advance both democratization and conflict management. This approach emphasizes the importance of choosing an appropriate electoral system to promote inclusivity and power sharing. In chapter 2, Harvey Glickman links the concern with electoral systems to overall problems of conflict management and constitutional design in Africa's multiethnic societies, underscoring the possibilities and the limits of constitutional engineering.

Part II addresses an important debate over electoral system choice—in sum, whether a plurality or a proportional representation system is best for Africa—and the effects of such choices on conflict management. These chapters include a focus on the following questions:

- How do various types of electoral systems contribute to the mitigation or exacerbation of conflict, particularly ethnic conflict? What are the most important elements of electoral system design as they relate to conflict management through democratic institutions?
- What has been learned about the consequences of electoral system choice from the experiences of post–Cold War elections in Africa?

Joel D. Barkan, in chapter 3, argues that majoritarian systems—winner-take-all, or first-past-the-post, arrangements—are best suited to African society because they offer a direct constituency-representative link, and that these systems can promote integrative, moderating effects across ethnic group lines. Majoritarian electoral systems, Andrew Reynolds rebuts in chapter 4, induce more competitive, confrontational, exclusionary politics, whereas proportional systems are often argued to produce inclusive, consensual governments.

Shaheen Mozaffar reports in chapter 5 on his empirical assessment of the arguments presented by Barkan and Reynolds using data on the post–Cold War elections in Africa. He argues that electoral system choice does have a strong effect on outcomes (such as the nature of the party system), and that therefore it has important implications for conflict management.

Part III focuses on Ghana and South Africa. These states' experiences with democratization and conflict management typify some of the broader questions that arise in the debate about the efficacy of elections and electoral system choice. In chapter 6, Emmanuel Gyimah-Boadi diagnoses the conflict management features of the 1996 election in Ghana, which is believed to have been a successful means of further inculcating democracy and multiethnic cooperation in that country.

In chapter 7, Robert B. Mattes and Amanda Gouws challenge a common assumption in the entire debate about elections and conflict management: that voting in a multiethnic society is tantamount to an ethnic census, that people overwhelmingly vote for those candidates or parties who share a similar identity rather than choosing on the basis of other issues, such as economic policy or the performance of incumbents. Using public opinion data from South Africa's celebrated 1994 election that ended the apartheid system, Mattes and Gouws argue that the "ethnic census" assumption deserves reconsideration. Voting behavior was not tantamount to an ethnic census, they contend.

If the progress toward greater democratization and conflict resolution in Africa is to be sustained, and if future mishaps are to be avoided, policymakers at many levels will need to consider carefully the effects of their decisions regarding elections on the exacerbation or mitigation of conflict. What some policymakers may perceive as a relatively technical issue—over an aspect of the electoral system such as district magnitude (the number of candidates to be elected per voting district), for example—may in fact turn out to have very important consequences for the success of the election and for peace and stability. Part IV, or chapter 8, assesses the policy implications of knowledge and experience accumulated from the remarkable wave of elections in Africa in recent years. This chapter explores the following questions:

- What are the inherent problems with elections in Africa? Given these problems, what are the critical choices, dilemmas, and trade-offs of international intervention that advocates elections as an instrument of political change?
- What can external parties, acting as mediators, do to promote more meaningful elections in Africa that simultaneously serve the aims of enhanced democratization and better conflict management?

The essays in this volume seek to help bridge the gap between the extensive scholarship on elections, electoral systems, and democratization and conflict management in Africa and the policies adopted by states, contestants in elections, and other external parties such as international and nongovernmental organizations. The details of electoral administration and electoral system design, no matter how arcane or technically laborious they may appear, are relevant for policymakers. These choices may be seen as the purview of scholarly or technical experts and not of diplomats and mediators, whose main concern is inducing parties to trade the bullet for the ballot. This view is misguided. Electoral systems and other issues related to electoral administration have tremendous effects on whether democratization and conflict management are advanced simultaneously, whether one goal is advanced at the expense of the other, or whether any given election entails a setback in the pursuit of both aims.

The editors would most like to thank the contributors to the volume and the participants at the June 1995 symposium for their thoughtful contributions to this collective research project. We mourn the passing of Claude Ake, who died in a tragic plane crash not long after the symposium. The staff and management at the United States Institute of Peace deserve our thanks for their support of this project and volume from its inception. Rhonda Blair and April Hall, especially, were instrumental in organizing the symposium, and Cynthia Benjamins of the Institute of Peace Press has been a supportive editor and valued manager of the publication process. David Smock, coordinator of the Institute's Africa activities, has been an ongoing adviser on the project and offered careful, insightful suggestions on the manuscript for which we are thankful. Two anonymous external reviewers for the Institute Press offered exceptionally valuable and critical suggestions for revision. Editorial coordination occurred during Timothy Sisk's tenure as a visiting fellow of the Norwegian Nobel Institute in Oslo, and he appreciates the Institute's support of his scholarship during that time. Andrew Reynolds thanks the Jennings Randolph fellowship program of the United States Institute of Peace for its support of his dissertation research, which is related to the theme of this volume, and the National Science Foundation (SBR-9321864) for its support of related research on constitutional design in Southern Africa.

# ■ PART I: Constitutional Engineering

The essays in part I provide an overview of the scholarly debate about the relationships between elections and conflict resolution in Africa. These chapters address the important theoretical questions of the linkages among elections, electoral systems, and conflict management.

In chapter 1, the editors take the position that elections can play myriad roles in creating the structures for pursuing politics without a turn to violence. The chapter also provides a primer on various electoral systems and argues that the choices among these systems have important implications for the types of political culture—consensual or competitive, inclusive or exclusive—that these systems help create.

# ELECTIONS AND ELECTORAL SYSTEMS
## Implications for Conflict Management

Andrew Reynolds and Timothy D. Sisk

There is a growing sense in both academic and policy circles that the promotion of rapid democratization in Africa at the beginning of the 1990s—with its emphasis on competitive, multiparty elections—was misguided at best, a fundamental mistake at worst. Democratization, we increasingly hear, more often than not unleashes forces of ethnic nationalism and generates new, deadly conflicts or catalyzes and stimulates ethnic enmities long submerged by the overarching ideological contest of the Cold War era. In short, Western governments are pulling back from their diplomatic and philanthropic pursuits of democratization in Africa, preferring to foster stability.

Some recent scholarship supports such thinking. New empirical analysis suggests that while mature democracies may be prone to conflict avoidance (Russet 1993), democratizing states are actually prone to both external (or international) and internal (or civil) violence. Edward Mansfield and Jack Snyder, for example, assert that "rising nationalism often goes hand in hand with rising democracy. . . . This concoction of nationalism and incipient democratization has been an intoxicating brew" (1995: 83, 85). The result is the propensity of manipulative elites in democratizing states to foment ethnic tensions for their own narrow, power-seeking pursuits, leading inexorably to external and internal wars as virulent nationalism sharply distinguishes between "we" and "they" and sets the stage for violent intergroup strife.[1]

Other studies suggest a mixed bag of experience with regard to the effects of democratization on ethnic conflict. Renee de Nevers argues that "democratization can prevent or dampen ethnic conflicts if the forces pushing for democratization, first, recognize and acknowledge the ethnic differences that exist within the state, and, second, if they can accommodate the interest of different groups in a way that is even handed. Neither is automatic" (1993: 61). In this view, the correlation between democratization and violent conflict, and especially ethnic conflict, is highly contingent. That is, whether democratization ameliorates or exacerbates conflict depends on myriad variables.

These broader arguments find an echo in the literature on democratization in Africa. Harvey Glickman (1995: i–ii) writes that "Ethnic and sectional conflict, hidden and often forcibly repressed by African regimes, wells up as politics becomes freer, and as competitive elections occur, not as repetitions of ancient blood feuds (a favorite newspaper phrase), but as strategies of political combat, which erupt into violence in the absence of institutional arrangements to distribute rewards."

African states, as pointed out in the introduction and highlighted throughout this book, have had a wide variety of experiences with democratization and with competitive, multiparty elections. Some efforts at democratization, especially inaugural or founding elections, have gone seriously awry; others have indisputably forwarded the twin causes of democratization and conflict resolution simultaneously. Elections have had both salutary and destructive effects on ethnic relations. Thus, it seems appropriate to recognize that democratization processes can go either way: they can serve to reconstitute a legitimate government and channel participation and contestation through inclusive, rule-governed institutions of the state, thereby opening up new opportunities for conflict management; or, they can establish the context for heightened tensions, fears, and, ultimately, widespread violence, especially but not inevitably along ethnic lines. One of the aims of this book is to highlight this important fact.

In this chapter, we assert the contingent approach of the relationship between democratization and conflict resolution and argue that, in the course of democratization, political actors make critically important choices over alternative institutions through which to manifest the transition toward democracy.[2] These choices, particularly the choice of an electoral system and the consequences of this choice for the democratization process, portend much for whether any given experience with democratization will exacerbate conflict or ameliorate it. Myriad other factors affect the extent to which the intoxicating brew to which Mansfield and Snyder refer will be concocted, but we place an analytical premium on the role of institutional design, and particularly on the role of elections and the systems under which they are contested in the democratization and conflict management processes.

In this chapter, we provide a theoretical point of departure for the essays that follow by identifying the underlying arguments that support the contingent approach to the nexus between democratization and conflict management. We also define key terms and perspectives on these admittedly complex issues and refer readers to the best literature on the subject. The focus on the effects of institutional choice supports the view that democratization and conflict resolution are not inevitably trade-offs, or that conflict resolution should be promoted as a short-term alternative to democratization. Rather, the critical question for both research and policy is how democratization can be conceived to achieve both aims concurrently. We do not agree with a dichotomy that juxtaposes democratic elections and social stability. On the contrary, elections can help create an environment that promotes social stability through the creation of legitimate, inclusive, representative governments.

## Democratization and Conflict Management: The Role of Elections

Elections must be viewed in context. They are neither the sole means nor the exclusive end of democracy. Moreover, the elections process is often misperceived as a rather simple, single-moment, horse race-type event—the actual balloting and the intriguing issue of who "wins" and who "loses"—rather than as a varied set of events and decisions leading up to elections that have long-lasting consequences once the proverbial dust has settled. Whether an election fosters the twin goals of democratization and conflict management depends upon many variables that are part and parcel of efforts at democratization and conflict management but are not directly related to the balloting itself.

Particularly in societies where current or previous conflicts were armed and militarized, the critical factors in elections are the extent to which armed factions contesting the elections are demilitarized, demobilized, and disarmed. When armed factions retain their ability to disrupt or repute the electoral outcome, elections are an exceptionally risky venture. This was the critical lesson of Angola's failed election in 1992 (Ohlson and Stedman 1994). Other factors are critical as well, such as the existence and development of a vibrant civil society; the level of sophistication and training of political parties; the economic context of development, especially the status of trade and investment liberalization and the presence or absence of structural adjustment policies; and the regional climate in which an election takes place.

Nevertheless, an election event is a defining moment—a critical turning point[3]—in any transition, with clear and important ramifications for whether the outcomes will lead to greater democracy and new opportunities of managing political conflict through political institutions. Skeptics of the importance placed on elections are correct that they are but a brief episode in a larger political process—moments in a transition in which what comes before and what comes after are equally important. But even as a brief episode, they are what can fruitfully be called linchpin events, in which progress toward greater democracy is made or set back, and in which the incentives and the disincentives for violent conflict, especially ethnic conflict, are rearranged and redefined. This is especially true of founding elections, which occur as the capstone of extended transitions from authoritarian rule to multiparty democracy (O'Donnell and Schmitter 1986), or as the crowning event of a protracted peace process that seeks to end a civil war and reestablish the legitimacy and authority of the state.

Elections are important to understand because, as Donald Rothchild suggests, they "direct our attention to both the transitions to democracy and the maintenance of democratic systems, once they are established."[4] As is noted above, both transitions to democracy and democratic consolidation have important ramifications for conflict management: transitions offer an opportunity to move away from violent conflict; consolidation allows a nation to institutionalize bargaining as a permanent, durable alternative to violence.

Political scientists generally agree that elections serve multiple roles in a democracy, more or less simultaneously, and they recognize that elections serve limited, but critical, purposes in the political process. First and foremost, of course, they seek to determine the will of the people. But David Butler, summing up the scholarly consensus on the purposes of elections, highlights that this aim is somewhat problematic.

> What do elections decide? There are some grounds for skepticism about their actual impact. Democracy only works when there is a fairly broad consensus about most of the national goals. Therefore, when elections lead to a change in the composition of governments the change seems often to be of men rather than of measures. . . . Elections decide less than most people suppose. Yet they give life and flexibility to the political system. There are grounds for anxiety about the electoral process, but not for despair [Butler 1987: 192].

Two separate typologies reflect the many roles that elections can play in a democratizing environment with the companion aim of promoting conflict management. The first deals broadly with the multiple role of elections in democracies generally; the second deals more specifically with the potential roles of elections in promoting the peaceful management of conflicts. In any democracy, elections can serve the following aims:

- *Legitimating rule: the will of the people.* The imprimatur of the support of the will of the people (or at least a plurality or majority of the people) is widely seen as the vehicle through which the ability to govern is legitimated. Robert Dahl, a preeminent theorist of democracy, writes,

> As an ostensible ideal, a component of prevailing ideologies, and a justificatory myth for rules, "democracy" has become nearly universal today. In authoritarian countries, in an attempt to lend legitimacy to the regime, "democracy" is often simply redefined.

Yet however much they distort and qualify the idea of democracy, in all except a handful of countries today government leaders not only claim that their government is for the good of the
people, as leaders tend to claim everywhere and always; but
beyond that, in most countries they also claim to be responsive
to the will of the people [1989: 233].

- *Alternation in the governing coalition and ruling elites.* In situations in which the defeat of an incumbent is possible, elections
  allow for alternation in governing coalitions. That is, today's
  officeholders may be tomorrow's opposition, and vice versa.
  Alternation in governing coalitions entails, essentially, an exchange of elites. Such an exchange may occur when a governing party is defeated and an opposition party takes over, or
  when leadership change occurs within a given government or
  party as a result of an election. Moreover, alternation and exchange of elites is viewed as healthy and necessary in inducing
  fresh ideas to governance and specific approaches to public
  policies (Horowitz 1991; Przeworski 1991).

The possibility of alternation is what keeps parties committed to
playing by the rules of the game: it institutionalizes uncertainty,
which is viewed as healthy precisely because it provides incentives
for continued play within the rules, as opposed to violently arbitrated conflicts in the streets. Donald Rothchild comments that "elections represent . . . the shadow of the future. If you feel you have
a chance of winning someday, then one may have a motive to play
according to the rules, and this encourages an ongoing democratic
process." Naturally, in situations of potential conflict along ethnic
group lines, alternation ensures that, potentially, no group is per-
manently excluded from power, which some analysts would argue
is a critical indicator of whether violence is likely (Gurr 1993).

- *Confidence-building.* If structured appropriately, elections provide incentives for political minorities to participate if they feel
  they have a chance of playing a significant role in the political
  life of a country; that is, elections give minorities the opportunity to exert influence and build confidence in the institutions.
- *Encouraging stability.* To the extent that elections are perceived
  as yielding representation, inclusiveness, and fairness, they foster

identification with and an ownership of the political system. The more a political system is perceived as representative, inclusive, fair, and just, the less the likelihood that any group of citizens will mobilize to change it violently. A key value is the legitimacy of the regime; stability based on order imposed by an illegitimate regime is illusory.

- *Educating the public.* Elections also serve a public education function by defining the issues, ideologies, and public policy positions of the contestants. Election campaigns force would-be rulers to articulate a vision for the society and to distinguish that vision from the visions of competitors. Elections offer significant opportunities for learning about the stated intent of parties to wield power as elected decisionmakers and about the personalities and views of any given candidate. Elections serve as an agent of social communication.

Similarly, one can posit the many roles of elections in fostering conflict management, particularly in recent years.

- *Inaugurating a post-conflict order.* Elections are, almost reflexively, perceived as the mechanism by which a transition from armed conflict to inclusive governance is accomplished. They are seen as the critical turning point at which a society moves from open, antagonistic violence to a new era based on bargaining and reciprocity. The more an election's outcome removes the incentives for violent opposition to the state, the greater the sense that the election has been successful in promoting conflict management.

- *Staving off impending conflict.* Elections serve conflict-management aims when their absence would entail the likelihood of a slide into violent conflict because of the illegitimacy or poor performance of the incumbent regime. That is, elections can serve a preemptive or preventive function with regard to violent conflict when the expectation exists that without a reconstitution of the political order, political violence is imminent.

- *Broadening the base of representation.* When the source of violent conflict is the sustained or permanent exclusion of a party or group from political power, elections—if properly structured—

can serve to broaden the base of political participation and allow for an expansion of the franchise or of representation.

In summarizing the roles of elections in terms of both democratization and conflict management, a simple fact should be underscored. Elections, as competitions among individuals, parties, and their ideas, are inherently just that: competitive. Elections are, and are meant to be, polarizing; they seek to highlight social choices. On the other hand, conflict management implies consensus-building, or reaching common ground. Is there an inherent tension between the competitive nature of elections and the consensus-seeking demands of conflict management? We suggest that the answer to the question is, "It depends." Perhaps the most important thing it depends on is the choices the parties make in the course of democratization and especially in negotiated transitions, about the types of political institutions to be employed, including, but not exclusively, the electoral system.

Institutions, which are in essence rule systems (March and Olsen 1989), are susceptible to "political engineering," or structuring of the rules of the game to provide incentives for specific types of behavior (Sartori 1968, 1994). If ethnic conflict is a danger to democratizing and even fully democratic states, political engineering can help mitigate conflicts. That is, the rules of the political game can be structured to offer incentives for moderation on divisive ethnic themes, to contain the destructive tendencies, and to preempt the centrifugal thrust created by ethnic politics. We do not claim that deft political engineering can prevent or eradicate deep enmities—that, for example, a cleverly constructed electoral system can manage to promote accommodation in a deeply conflicted, ethnically unbalanced society like Rwanda, where the now-dominant Tutsi population is but 14 percent of the total population—but that appropriate institutions can nudge the political system in the direction of reduced conflict and greater governmental accountability in many instances. The common assumption is that choices about the basic rules of the game affect its outcomes. Horowitz notes, "Where there is some determination to play by the rules, the rules can restructure the system so the game itself changes" (1985: 601).

## Electoral Systems and Conflict Management: A Primer

The set of democratic institutions a nation adopts is integral to the long-term success of any new regime as it structures the rules of the game of political competition. Moreover, the process by which these institutions are adopted is equally important. How inclusive and legitimate is the constitution-making process? Within the constitution-making process, few choices are as important as which electoral system is to be used, because this single institution will help determine what parties look like, who is represented in parliament, and ultimately who governs. This is why electoral system design has been seized upon by many scholars (Horowitz 1991; Lijphart 1977 and 1984; Reynolds 1993 and 1995a, 1995b, and 1995c; and Sartori 1968, 1994) as one of the chief levers of constitutional engineering to be used in mitigating conflict within divided societies. As Lijphart notes, "If one wants to change the nature of a particular democracy, the electoral system is likely to be the most suitable and effective instrument for doing so" (Lijphart 1995: 412).

An electoral system is designed to do three main jobs. First, it will translate the votes cast into seats won in a legislative chamber. The system may give more weight to proportionality (so that the disparity between a political party's vote share and its seat share is not great), or it may funnel the votes (however fragmented among parties) into a parliament that contains two large parties representing polarized views. Second, any electoral system seeks to be the conduit through which the people can hold their elected representatives accountable. Third, the system has a more normative function, to structure the boundaries of "acceptable" political discourse and give incentives for those competing for power (political parties) to couch their appeals to the electorate in distinct ways. For example, some electoral systems may encourage parties to make chauvinistic appeals to "their" group, which may appear as hostile and exclusionary appeals to "other" groups, while other electoral systems reward those parties that make broadly based, inclusive appeals for support. However, the "spin" that an electoral system gives to the system is ultimately contextual and will depend on the specific cleavages and divisions within any given society.

The main electoral system choices are between plurality-majority systems and proportional representation systems. Plurality-majority systems most often use single member districts. In a plurality (or *first-past-the-post*) system, the winner is the candidate with the most votes, not necessarily an absolute majority of the votes (50 percent plus one). In majoritarian systems, such as the Australian *alternative vote* and the French *two-ballot system,* the winning candidate must receive an absolute majority. In essence, both majoritarian systems use second preferences to produce an absolute majority winner if no one emerges in the first round of voting. Although no African state has adopted the alternative vote, several—especially francophone countries—have inherited or adopted the French two-ballot system.

The underpinning rationale of all proportional representation (PR) systems is to reduce the disparity between a party's share of the national votes and its share of the parliamentary seats. For example, if a major party wins 40 percent of the votes, it should win approximately 40 percent of the seats; and likewise, a minor party with 10 percent should also gain roughly a tenth of the parliamentary seats. Proportionality is best approximated by using lists, where political parties present a list of candidates to the voters, or the *single transferable vote*, where voters rank candidates numerically in multimember districts. The formula used to calculate the allocation of seats after the votes have been counted can also have a marginal effect.[5]

Of more importance to overall PR results are district size (or district magnitude) and the threshold for representation. The larger the districts and the lower the imposed "threshold of representation," the more proportional the electoral system will be and the greater chance small parties will have of gaining representation. For example, in Israel the imposed threshold is 1 percent, in Germany it is 5 percent, and in the Seychelles in 1993 a 9 percent threshold was imposed for the PR seats. In South Africa in 1994 there was no legal threshold for representation, and the African Christian Democratic Party won two seats with only 0.45 percent of the national vote. Other important choices involve how district boundaries are drawn; how parties constitute their PR lists; the complexity of the ballot paper (the range of choice given to the voter—between parties, or between candidates and parties); the size of parliament; and arrangements for electoral, "vote-pooling," coalitions between parties (known as *apparentement*).

To date, pure first-past-the-post or plurality single-member-district (SMD) systems are often found in the United Kingdom and the countries it influenced. In Africa, Botswana, Gambia, Ghana, Kenya, Lesotho, Malawi, São Tome and Principe, Zambia, and Zimbabwe all use single member district plurality systems. Zimbabwe used a list PR system for its independence elections of 1980, but in the three elections since 1985 it has used an SMD plurality system.

List PR systems are the electoral systems most frequently used in democracies and they are becoming increasingly common. More than twenty established democracies use some variant of list PR, with seats allocated within a number of regionally based districts, while Germany, Israel, and the Netherlands award seats on the basis of a single nationwide district (Lijphart 1994). In Africa, Benin, Burkina Faso, Burundi, Madagascar, Mozambique, and Niger follow the district-based list PR model, while Angola and Senegal join Namibia and South Africa in calculating seats at the national level.

Ideally, any electoral system should fulfill the following key criteria that influence the quality of democracy and prospects for good governance. However, it must be noted that these criteria may not always be mutually compatible and that different electoral systems will do better in some categories than others. In both ethnically divided and more homogeneous societies, trade-offs have to be made among a number of competing normative ends:

- *Representativeness.* In order to be legitimate and credible, and to maximize electoral consent, the electoral system needs to fairly reflect the opinions of the electorate, and not just the majority, because parliament needs to be seen to reflect the composition of society along ethnic, regional, and other (such as urban-rural) lines.

- *Accountability.* The government and elected members of parliament must be accountable to their constituents to the highest degree possible. This level of accountability involves more than merely holding regular national elections. Accountability also depends upon the degree of geographical accountability (the size and territorial nature of constituencies) and the level of choice between candidates as well as parties.

- *Inclusiveness and accessibility.* The legislature will be representative only to the extent that people do not feel alienated and excluded from the political process. If citizens feel their vote makes a difference in elections, they are far more likely to exercise their democratic rights and even participate beyond the simple walk to the polling station once every five years. Accessibility to the political process through the electoral system does not imply just the representation of minority groups; it also relates to the degree of difficulty less educated or illiterate voters encounter in the polling booth.

- *Stability of government.* The electoral system needs to interpret the will of the people if it is to create a government that has the authority that stems from the support of the majority of the electorate. An electoral system is successful only if it gives rise to governments that are capable of enacting legislation, maintaining order, and being sensitive to shifts in public opinion. Any system adopted should also promote a viable parliamentary opposition grouping that can critically assess government legislation and safeguard minority rights.

- *Development of the party system.* The electoral system should be designed to encourage the development of parties that are based on ideological-political values and specific policy programs rather than on ascriptive (ethnic or regional) cleavages. It is clear from the evidence that party systems based on socioeconomic or ideological cleavages are more enduring and stable than those based on ethnicity.

- *Ability to engender reconciliation.* Throughout Africa it is crucial that all institutions are designed to facilitate an environment of reconciliation. This does not necessarily mean enforced consensus but, rather, the mutual recognition of opposing views in the political system. Any system that exaggerates adversarial and confrontational politics will perpetuate the divisions that exist within many fledgling democracies and retard the building of unified and cohesive nation states.

With these criteria in mind, what are the cited advantages and disadvantages of various electoral systems for conflict management and good governance in Africa?

### Plurality/SMD

Many advocates of a plurality SMD system believe that the system has properties that would be beneficial to fledgling democracies in Africa. They contend that

- Plurality offers the electorate a clear-cut choice between two broadly based competing parties, and the national vote clearly translates into winning and losing parties. Under PR, no single party may have enough seats to govern alone, and so shifting coalitions effectively take the choice of government out of the voters' hands and place it in the arms of negotiating party bosses.

- This clear-cut choice (and the "seat bonuses" inherent in plurality SMD) gives rise to single-party executives who are deemed to be more effective at protecting new democracies from gridlock, impotence, and ineffectiveness at the time of most pressing need.

- The dynamics of electoral competition when there are two large parties requires political elites to mobilize around broadly inclusive and politically moderate issues that reflect a socioeconomic divide as opposed to a cultural or territorial divide. When there is no overwhelmingly dominant group, parties have to cobble together coalitions of disparate interest groups under plurality SMD.

- While the system does produce single-party cabinets, plurality SMD also facilitates strong parliamentary oppositions, which provide a checking role on the government of the day and position themselves as administrations-in-waiting.

- The way in which plurality discriminates against minority parties (either through parliamentary underrepresentation or through complete exclusion) curtails the destabilizing impact of tiny extremist parties. In this respect, the inclusiveness of PR is a drawback of the system.[6]

- Single-member districts preserve the vertical link between constituent and representative that is lost once larger multimember districts are brought into play. If members of parliament have a defined geographical area for which they, and they alone, are responsible, they will have a closer affinity with their district, be more combative on its behalf, and be held to a higher level of accountability.
- In societies that are unfamiliar with democratic practice and that suffer high levels of illiteracy, the simplicity of plurality's single "X" vote is perceived to be a major advantage.
- "Real" democracy equates to Westminster-style majoritarianism, of which a plurality SMD is an integral part.

In response, critics of plurality argue that its ethos of exclusion, on a number of levels, can be fatal in divided societies where there is no real consensus on institutionalized competition for control of the state. These critics contend that

- Plurality excludes minority parties who may prove to be a more destabilizing presence outside the political system than they would have been if incorporated into structures of political representation.
- If voting behavior dovetails with ethnic divisions, ethnic minority group members may well be excluded from parliamentary representation, which can be destabilizing for the political system as a whole.
- Cross-country evidence shows that women are far less likely to be elected to parliament under plurality systems than under PR systems.
- Plurality provides incentives for the mobilization of ethnic divisions. The system tends to create "regional fiefdoms" in which one party, through winning a majority of votes in the region, wins all, or nearly all, of the parliamentary seats, excluding minorities from access to representation.
- Relating to this is the prevalence of "wasted votes," where minority party supporters begin to feel that they have no realistic hope of ever electing a candidate of their choice. This can increase alienation from the political system and the likelihood

that extremists will be able to mobilize antisystem movements. In Africa, approximately one-fifth of votes are wasted under plurality SMD systems, while only 2 to 5 percent are wasted under PR systems.

- The pattern of geographically concentrated electoral support in Africa means that one party can maintain exclusive executive control in the face of a substantial drop in popular support. Under plurality, a party may fall from 60 to 40 percent of the popular vote nationally, but in the seats it holds this may represent a fall from 80 to 60 percent, which does not affect its overall seat-winning potential. Unless seats are highly competitive, the system is insensitive to swings in public opinion.

- Single-member district systems are particularly open to manipulation by ruling parties who can gerrymander boundaries to their own advantage.

### Proportional Representation

In many respects, the strongest arguments for PR emanate from the way in which the system avoids the anomalous results of plurality and facilitates a more "representative" legislature.

- It is far easier for minority parties to gain parliamentary representation under PR, and this acts as an important confidence-building mechanism, assuaging a minority's fear that it will be submerged in the new democratic order.

- PR encourages parties, both large and small, to constitute regionally, ethnically, and gender-diverse lists as they need to appeal to a wide spectrum of individuals to maximize their overall national vote. There are fewer incentives to make ethnically exclusive appeals for support, which in turn breeds hostility.

- Perhaps the strongest evidence linking electoral system design to conflict mitigation in Africa is that PR avoids the vagaries of the "Anglo-American" plurality SMD, that often gives large seat bonuses and manufactured parliamentary majorities to parties which have won only a plurality of the popular vote, and sometimes have won fewer votes than their opponents.[7]

• PR reduces the problems of wasted votes and regional fiefdoms outlined above. When PR has been used in Africa, very few regions, or districts, have been monopolized by representatives of a single party.

• The coalition governments generated by PR electoral systems are more reflective of the realities of African states. Decisions are made in open government, rather than behind closed doors, between those who hold political power and those who retain economic control (whites in South Africa, Zimbabwe, and to some extent Namibia). Nevertheless, as was implied in the earlier "advantages of plurality" section, on the negative side PR creates legislative gridlock at the time of most pressing need, allows tiny minority parties to hold larger parties for ransom in coalition negotiations, and mitigates against the building of nonculturally rooted, broadly based political parties that have a shot at winning government outright.

### The Alternative Vote in Multimember Districts (the Horowitz Proposal)

For the purposes of this introduction to electoral systems, it is useful to go beyond the straight plurality versus PR divide and evaluate the properties of a majoritarian system, the alternative vote in multimember districts, which was proposed for the new South African constitution by Donald Horowitz. Although a rarely used electoral system, this proposal received widespread attention in both the United States and Africa. Leroy Vail of Harvard University speculated that Horowitz's ideas "might well shape the outcome of discussions in South Africa regarding the country's future" (Horowitz 1991: dust jacket). In *A Democratic South Africa? Constitutional Engineering in a Divided Society* (1991), Horowitz argued that "the incentive to compromise, and not merely the incentive to coalesce," is the key to accommodation in an ethnically divided society (Horowitz 1991: 171). This argument rested on the empirically well-founded premise that parliamentary coalitions between differing ethnic parties often fall apart because there is no substantive common-interest glue to keep them together (Lipset 1979).

Horowitz therefore argued that incentives for pre-election compromise that encouraged "vote-pooling" or party appeals across ethnic boundaries are key to crafting a stable and less ethnically divisive constitutional order. He envisaged a system in which parties would have to bargain with the voters by offering concessions on ethnic and social matters. And for the parliamentary opposition to dislodge the government, it would have to outbid the governing coalition at being moderate.

In practical terms, he argued that these incentives would be engendered by the alternative vote, which forces the winning candidate in a district to win an absolute majority of the votes (50 percent plus one). If no one candidate wins more than 50 percent of the first preferences, the lowest polling candidate is eliminated, and his or her second preferences are redistributed to candidates remaining in the race. This process continues until a single candidate surmounts the 50 percent threshold. However, these incentives only kick in if no one party has an absolute majority of (or perceives it has an absolute majority of) the district's votes. As Horowitz himself noted, "If a party can win on first preferences, second preferences are irrelevant" (1991: 194). Because of the correlation of ethnicity, geographical concentration, and party preference in South Africa, Horowitz recognized that constituencies would have to be heterogeneous to allow for the possibility that no single party would win an absolute majority. "To achieve this [heterogeneity], the constituencies may have to be large, and they may therefore need to be multimember constituencies" (195).

In a detailed analysis of the Horowitz proposal, Arend Lijphart (1991) questioned the applicability of the alternative vote in multimember districts to South Africa and prophesied that the system would have disastrous implications for stability and democratization in South Africa if used in practice. Lijphart's critique rested on three main points. First, he said party coalitions within parliament carry incentives to compromise similar to vote-pooling incentives on the electoral level. Second, he said that the alternative vote, in theory and in practice, resembles the majority-runoff method that was found to be highly unsatisfactory when used in divided societies in 19th century Europe. He quotes an argument by Stein

Rokkan, "It was no accident that the earliest moves to proportional representation came in the ethnically most heterogeneous countries. . . . In linguistically and religiously divided societies majority elections could clearly threaten the continued existence of the political system. The introduction of some element of minority representation came to be seen as an essential step in a strategy of territorial consolidation" (Rokkan 1970: 157).

Third, Lijphart refuted Horowitz's claim that alternative voting would "mitigate the winner-take-all aspects of plurality systems" and that it would by necessity "achieve better proportionality of seats to votes than plurality systems do" (Horowitz 1991: 166). Lijphart noted that alternative voting operated in multimember constituencies to make the system even less proportional and more majoritarian. "In PR systems proportionality increases as district magnitude increases, but the relationship is just the other way round for majoritarian systems. AV's disproportionality will rise sharply when it is applied in multi-member districts." (Lijphart 1991: 96).[8]

### Fostering Inclusive Political Outcomes

As noted in the Introduction, political scientists believe that electoral system choice has important ramifications for the evolution of the party system and for the outcomes that flow from electoral competition. Just as institutions constitute just one (although integral) aspect of the socio-political-economic underpinnings of successful democratization and conflict management, electoral systems similarly exist as one cog in a wheel contingent upon the design of other influential institutions. Chief among these other democratic choices, which are related to elections, are issues of "democratic type," meaning the choice between majoritarian government, where one party may rule alone if it can muster enough seats in the legislature, and power-sharing structures, where governments of national unity are mandated to include all parties with "significant" electoral support. (In South Africa and Sierra Leone, parties with more than 5 percent of the assembly seats were awarded positions in the cabinet).[9] Also critical is the "executive type," meaning whether to have a directly elected president or prime minister whose legitimacy is based on his or her leadership of the largest party in the parliament. A final important factor is the degree of centralization of state power, meaning whether the constitution adopts a governing ethos of decentralization and federalism or its opposite, a centralized unitary state.

A clear pattern is emerging that suggests, contrary to apocalyptic predictions of Africa's degeneration into lawlessness, that those countries that adopt institutional mechanisms that create an atmosphere of inclusion are doing considerably better than the states that opted for structures with an exclusionary bent. Drawing on the lessons from these success stories, it has become widely accepted that the only realistic solutions for settling the horrific problems of the war-torn, divided societies of Africa are inclusive arrangements. Ann Reid of the U.S. State Department notes that "most of the African wars of the past thirty-five years of independence have roots in a winner-take-all approach to politics. One ethnic group or coalition of groups dominates an African government and excludes other groups, intensifying ethnic tensions and generating violence, [thus] the key to conflict resolution in a multiethnic African state is a political deal that gives a share of power to each of the major ethnic groups." Along with Sierra Leone, Mozambique was able to end its bloody civil war through institutional arrangements that were acceptable to both Frelimo (Front for the Liberation of Mozambique) and Renamo (Mozambique National Resistance).

This ethos of the political inclusion of both minorities and majorities in decision-making structures improves the prospects for peace and stability on a number of levels. It has most value as a confidence-building mechanism that allows both political elites and cultural/ethnic communities to feel that they have influence on the decisions of the state and that their representatives will be able to ensure that their rights are protected. Such confidence building was made visible in the multiethnic and multiracial "rainbow" cabinets of South Africa (1994–1996) and Namibia. The South African government of national unity included cabinet ministers of Zulu, Xhosa, Tswana, white (both English and Afrikaner), coloured and Indian background. At the time of the National Party's withdrawal in May 1996, two of President Nelson Mandela's African

National Congress ministers were white, and Deputy President F. W. De Klerk's National Party ministers included one black and one coloured. The same was true in the early years of democracy in Namibia, where President Sam Nujoma went out of his way to appoint cabinet ministers from outside his Ovambo ethnic base. Such familiarity breeds accommodation. Bernard Grofman has noted that in the United States, "the presence of [racial] minority office-holders makes it harder for racism to persist inside a legislature," and throughout democracies, "the simple presence of members of one's own group in government is an important symbol of equality and full citizenship" (Grofman 1994).

Inclusive structures not only build confidence in divided societies, they facilitate a better distribution of resources from the center to the country as a whole, while democracies with exclusionary institutions create an incentive for ruling parties to pamper their home region or ethnic group to the detriment of the numerically smaller population groups who lose out in the electoral fray. Such is the case in Malawi, where a north-south regional axis, of the southern-based United Democratic Front (UDF) and the northern-based Alliance for Democracy (AFORD) adroitly excluded the central region, dominated by the Malawi Congress Party, the former one-party regime headed by Hastings Banda, from development grants. With the instability of the UDF-AFORD coalition, the situation may get even worse, with a minority UDF government excluding both the central and northern regions from future resource allocations.

Inclusive coalition governments also make long-term structural adjustment programs more feasible because all significant interests are committed to the project from the start, and thus it becomes more difficult for them to destabilize the process down the road. Nevertheless, at the end of the day the most persuasive argument for power-sharing structures is that the alternative is nearly always a catastrophic breakdown of the state and society. Whether it be in Angola, Namibia, Rwanda, Sierra Leone, Somalia, or South Africa, the failure to respect and reassure all significant component parts of the nation has resulted in bloody conflict. Only in Botswana has majoritarian democracy endured, and this is the result of the unusual homogeneity of the Tswana population and the way in which Seretse Khama, and later Ketumile Masire, at the helm of a strong but ethnically neutral state, managed to bypass winner-take-all electoral structures to incorporate local leaders and powerful interest groups. Even so, government has never changed hands in Botswana (one of Donald Horowitz's prerequisites for a robust democracy), and the opposition has been seriously disadvantaged by the electoral system for more than thirty years. In Liberia and Mozambique, winner-take-all presidential elections have resulted in initially stable regimes, although clearly failure to rule inclusively could return those societies to war (especially in Liberia).

It is true that there have been constitutional settlements that attempted to facilitate a degree of inclusion but that failed to bring about long-term political stability or democratic consolidation—for example in Angola, Burundi, Liberia, Rwanda, and Zimbabwe (in 1992). But each of these settlements was flawed in at least one important respect. In Zimbabwe, uncontrollable ethnic conflict has been avoided to date, but democracy has withered, and there has been suppression of human rights and erosion of the institutions of civil society. For its first nonracial elections, in 1980, Zimbabwe used a combination of proportional representation (for the common roll) and twenty reserved seats for whites in an attempt to protect minority rights and reassure white business interests. But after he took power, Robert G. Mugabe quickly moved to switch to a plurality SMD electoral system, remove the incongruous whites-only seats, co-opt into government his chief opponent, Ndebele leader Joshua Nkomo, and suppress political opposition to his rule. By 1996, Mugabe had transformed Zimbabwe into a part de facto, part de jure one-party state that had become defined by the politics of exclusion.

The fatal flaw that allowed Zimbabwean democracy to ebb away was that the inclusive mechanism used to appease the fears of white "Rhodesians" was the promise of economic protection and influence (a mechanism that continues to be used) rather than the protection of political representation—the twenty reserved seats were never a serious threat to black majority political power. It was, in a sense, a kind of racially based corporatism. In contrast, when a powerful economic minority is able to extract political guarantees, as happened in South Africa and Namibia, there are spin-off benefits to other marginalized groups, mostly black, who do not have the leverage of financial muscle.

If a negotiated settlement amounts to institutionalized pluralism, as opposed to corporatism, the whole society benefits. In South Africa, the PR electoral system and government of national unity, which were given as negotiating chips to the National Party, ultimately benefited the Zulu-based Inkatha Freedom Party, the liberal white Democratic Party, the Afrikaner Freedom Front, and the black nationalist Pan-Africanist Congress of Azania. Similarly, in Namibia, the concessions gained by the Democratic Turnhalle Alliance allowed the Damara-based United Democratic Front and a number of other minor parties to gain representation. Those benefits have not been made available to nonwhite opposition groups in Zimbabwe. Despite huge obstacles to their participation, these groups consistently get one-fifth of the popular vote but in the last two elections they have been reduced to a total of three (out of 150) parliamentary seats as a result of the exclusionary electoral system.

Furthermore, while buying off one minority with economic influence does create a type of power sharing, it is an unaccountable, undemocratic, and secretive method of sharing power.[10] It enables elites to skim the pot while the impoverished masses continue to be excluded from a fair allocation of resources. In contrast, if the power sharing is politically entrenched and based on parties that have proven electoral appeal, the electorate has a better chance to restrain the elites from the malignant cancer of corruption. As Victor Magagna has written (1988),

> Corporatism, in contrast to pluralism, restricts the meaning of popular sovereignty by equating the needs of the people with the public's obvious interest in economic growth. Corporatism may lead to a hegemonic discourse of the sovereign economy, and, in this sense, pluralism's openness to a plurality of discourses about the meaning of the public interest is closer to the democratic goal of a society of free and full public agreement.

Events in Liberia, Rwanda, and Angola illustrate that the structures of inclusion have to be complete and extensive for power-sharing solutions to work. For eight months before the chaotic events of April 1996, Liberia was governed by a transitional council led by three main faction leaders. That the council fell apart was in no small part testament to the fact that the international mediators who had brokered the Abuja agreement (that brought peace to Liberia) placed a high priority on the interests of certain combatants while overlooking the representation of other potentially violent groups and, perhaps most important, the peaceful Liberian majority. Liberia's disintegration was precipitated by the exclusion of D. Roosevelt Johnson, de facto leader of the Krahn ethnic group, from the council of state. As a result of this slap in the face, Johnson began to marshal alienated Krahn soldiers, many of whom were children, which prompted a preemptive strike by Charles Taylor's forces on Roosevelt's compound on April 6, 1996.

There is no doubt that the "warlords," typified by Taylor and Johnson, had to be included in the power-sharing structures, but by leaving out the stabilizing representatives of Liberian civil society— church groups, journalists, academics, businesspeople, and the judiciary—the mediators guaranteed that the interim arrangements would not lay the foundations for long-term stability. The 1997 election in Liberia, in which Taylor obtained the presidency in a winner-take-all outcome, suggests that peace in that country is on shaky ground. In neighboring Sierra Leone, civil society similarly and remarkably endured the years of conflict, but its leaders were brought in as partners in the negotiations that constructed the new constitutional dispensation.

The lesson from the divergent experiences of Liberia and Sierra Leone is that mere power sharing between those who make war is not enough. Either the constituent groups that come to the table need to have had their legitimacy tested at the ballot box, or the negotiations must include a wide spectrum of more obviously representative groups, as was the case in the negotiation councils that oversaw the transition to a democratic South Africa. Michael Chege argues that "the strongest hope for democracy in Africa" is the "politically committed and well-educated members of civic and opposition groups whose belief in the continent's capacity for better government is unshakable" (1995).

In Rwanda, President Juvénal Habyarimana attempted to play off hard-line Hutus in his own party against the Tutsi leaders of the insurgent Rwandan Patriotic Front (RPF). In August 1993, Habyarimana offered to transfer his power to a consensus cabinet made up of both Hutus and Tutsis, but a major Hutu extremist party was excluded from government, and the RPF clung to the belief that it could win everything in a zero-sum game if it could bring down the president. The excluded Hutu extremists felt increasingly threatened by the president's approaches to the Tutsi leaders, and in April 1994 they shot down the president's plane. The nation returned to the most extreme form of violent ethnic conflict, genocide.

Finally, U.S. State Department official Ann Reid notes that the collapse of the Bicesse peace accords in Angola stemmed from a failure to implement the whole range of accommodatory structures:

> The focus at Bicesse was elections, not power-sharing. The Angolan government constitution, which concentrated power in the presidency, remained in place, and both [José Eduardo] dos Santos and [Jonas] Savimbi competed for the only prize worth having. Although the legislature was elected by proportional representation, it was regarded as a rubber-stamp for presidential decisions. The two antagonists gave only lip service to a coalition government; after dos Santos' victory, he made a derisory offer of minor ministries to UNITA. Washington and Moscow each believed that its client would win the presidency. Little attention was given to the possibility that the loser would opt out of the political transition and resume fighting [Reid 1995].

Liberia, Rwanda, and Angola illustrate that most of the attempts at power sharing that failed have been deeply flawed. But, it must also be noted that sometimes—as in Somalia, Burundi, and Rwanda, and possibly Liberia—the pressures for violent conflict are just too strong, and the disintegration of society has gone too far, for power sharing to be successful. These countries are not hopeless, but they require stronger medicine than constitutional engineering can provide. Disarmament would be a good start. In the end, while appropriate constitutional arrangements are central to the politics of accommodation, they are not a panacea, and they can be overwhelmed by the most extreme forms of division, lawlessness, and societal breakdown.

## Conclusion

In the absence of evidence to show that one-party regimes are more favorable to economic, social, and political development than multiparty democratic regimes, choices have to be made among democratic institutions and structures. Since 1990, multiparty elections have been held in more than two-thirds of the sub-Saharan African states. Most important, it is becoming increasingly apparent, as Africa catches up on what Samuel P. Huntington (1991) calls the "third wave" of democratic transitions, that it is the "type of democracy" that most influences the success or failure of these fledgling regimes—not only the electoral institutions chosen to constitute parliaments and governments, legislatures and executives, but the powers these respective bodies are given.

Thus, there is wide agreement that inclusiveness is a prerequisite of ethnic accommodation and political stability, but there is far less agreement on which institutional arrangements best facilitate an aura of inclusion. Scholars such as Ian Shapiro and Courtney Jung (1995) have argued that the power-sharing arrangements of the interim South African constitution were a serious impediment to any progress toward a true democracy, and that without Westminster-style majoritarian institutions the South Africans would not have the "basic ingredients of a viable democracy." Arend Lijphart (1995b), on the other hand, has repeatedly advocated the benefits of precisely the power-sharing democracy so disparaged by Shapiro and Jung. Donald Horowitz has recommended the "nation-building" potential of directly elected presidents, whereas a number of other writers have characterized the presidential option as a disastrous recipe for ethnic minority exclusion and instability. Finally, many critics cite federalism for its consensual and conflict-resolving tendencies, while others see powerful regional governments as providing dangerous incentives to parties to mobilize ethnic or regional groups through hostile and nationally divisive appeals.

Although this volume deals principally with elections and electoral systems, the reader should bear in mind the multiplicity of choice when it comes to designing the rules of the political game in Africa, and the interconnectivity of institutions and their consequences for democratization and conflict management. As chapter 2 shows, Africa must overcome more than institutional problems if elections are to have the beneficial and meaningful effects we advocate.

# 2

# ETHNICITY, ELECTIONS, AND CONSTITUTIONAL DEMOCRACY IN AFRICA

Harvey Glickman

African politics remains severely divided by ethnic conflict. Quite apart from the dramatic events of Rwanda or Sudan or Liberia, where mass murder is enmeshed in perceived differences in ethnic identity, the political space provided by openings toward democracy in less than a decade remains an arena where policy debate competes unequally with ethnic appeals, ethnic parties, and ethnically based support for candidates. Transitions away from authoritarian rule in the 1990s offered some opportunities for multiethnic cooperation, often reflected in the national conference phenomenon in francophone countries (Robinson 1994: 578–600; Clarke 1995: 230–231, 250–252), but in the near term, and on the whole, they have had the opposite effect. While democracy of some vintage correlates with stable government, the process of democratizing is conflict-ridden (Ottaway 1995: 235–236; Lemarchand 1992: 98–100).

Africa is not alone in this respect. Ethnic conflicts have characterized the post–Cold War world. Grandiosely, Africa has been cast as a subset of "the clash of civilizations" (Huntington 1996a: 21–28, 268–272). Ethnic group sentiments—"tribalism"—have been recognized and exploited in the past in African authoritarian politics, most notably providing the major excuse for the suppression of popular expression, but serving also as a major path to patronage and influence, as "ethnic brokerage" (Welsh 1996: 486–487; Rothchild 1985: 72–73; Ihonvbere 1994a: 52–54; Chazan 1982). One can argue that today's ethnic conflict was stimulated in the era of state centralization, which encouraged minority elites to raise the ethnic standard to achieve rewards (Brass 1991: 8–9). Since few African states reflect one-nation self-determination or have had success in building one nation, multiple ethnonationalistic appeals must be expected in a period of political liberalization.

Ethnopolitics stands in an ambiguous relationship to democracy. On the one hand, ethnic and religious groups are agencies of resistance to centralized state exploitation of the masses. On the other hand, such groups are not democratically organized, indeed are sometimes agencies of fanaticism. So ethnonationalism poses a continuing threat to a democratization process, not only because of the hardening differences brought out by competitive discourse, but also because of the consummatory rather than pragmatic goals of ethnonationalism. Despite occasional official bans, it is an instrument of struggle within a political elite, as attested in voting support and in the arithmetic of cabinet formation, gaining strength as a result of its resonance with ties of place and kinship in rural communities. As a vein of "vertical solidarity," it reinforces clientelism and vice versa. But its effects can be diffused as it clashes with "competing veins of solidarity," such as class relations, the growing cosmopolitanism of urban youth and labor, and growing peasant entrepreneurship (Randrianja 1996: 33–35).

In the long march to democratic government, a respect for liberty and pluralism cannot bar the airing of cultural and social differences and appeals to ethnicity. Exhortations to moral individualism or civic patriotism do not eliminate pride in group identity. In the African context, there is precedent for the mobilization of ethnic sentiments in the short periods of open politics and a healthy respect for ethnic attachments when the system has been closed. Rather than expecting the elimination of ethnic conflict, the democratization process, stormy as it may be, means finding mechanisms to ameliorate it. Whatever the anthropological origins and nature of ethnicity in Africa, it is being put to instrumental uses in politics today (Eller and Coughlan 1993). Under appropriate conditions, ethnopolitics is amenable to bargaining (Glickman 1995: 6–9). Indeed there is a certain necessity to find such conditions, to preempt ethnic warfare by inviting bargaining practices before the buildup of antagonistic ethnic memories and before states collapse (Zartman 1995: 269–271). Such conditions permit ethnic representation or inclusion in state policy processes, encompassed in horizontal (territorial) federalism or vertical (functional) federalism. Whatever the labels, the point is to weaken the frontiers of ethnicity by reducing its salience or inducing ethnopolitical groups to cooperate (Randrianja 1996: 40–41).

A number of institutions, elections and electoral systems among them, permit the expression and demonstration of ethnic differences in constructive ways. Ethnic conflict is not incompatible with institutions of democratic government, when its expression is limited to a group interest among other interests, and if the means of expression provide openings to share rewards in a predictable manner. The argument here is that ethnic conflict, when it is openly competitive, is not always and need not always be deadly or violent, but can become a politically acceptable manifestation of the assertion and recognition of group rights. The issue of ethnic group competition in the present era of democratization is one of control, not elimination. Managing conflict—by channeling ethnic group conflict into nonviolent competition, by rewarding interethnic coalition making and the moderation of demands—that is the main challenge (Rothchild and Foley 1988; Rothchild 1991; Horowitz 1991, 1993).

Mechanisms to moderate ethnopolitical activity are in competition with the state-breaking threat of ethnonationalism (Coakley 1992). Polarized, politicized ethnicity challenges existing territorial boundaries, which remain perhaps the strongest legacy of colonial rule in Africa. In the long view, what is happening in Africa today is part of the larger process of the post-colonial reallocation of political authority. Distorted by the Cold War, which propped up military and one-party dictatorships, it was detoured by specious and centralized control of African economies. Few African states

were able to sustain competitive electoral systems after independence, largely because victorious political leaders barely tried.
Perhaps more important, the debate about possible homegrown
alternatives to the inherited electoral and representative systems
centered on nationalist movement unity or on the relevance of
traditional, supposedly consensual, political harmony to the territorial politics of independence (Glickman 1967: 195–200). The argument for political uniformity fit neatly with the putative relevance
of central state planning to economic development.

The first post-colonial international relations regime on the continent appeased successful territorial anticolonial ("nationalist")
leaders. With the two major exceptions of Tanzania and Eritrea
(and the minor and temporary one of Senegal-Mali), inherited territorial boundaries acquired sacrosanct status, enshrined in the
doctrine of the Organization of African Unity (OAU) from its founding. The civil wars and internal strife of the 1990s spill over into
neighboring states, undermine territorial sovereignty, threatening
governmental collapse or secession (Zartman 1995). Whether
Rwanda and Burundi can be made whole again remains an open
question. Since the victory of the TPLF-EPLF (Tigrayan People's
Liberation Front, Eritrean People's Liberation Front) in Ethiopia
led to the secession of Eritrea, a precedent has been set. Ethiopia
has embarked on an intriguing and risky experiment in establishing an ethnically based federation with the right of secession (Young
1996). Somalia today appears to be at least two political entities.
The unrecognized "republic" in northern Somaliland in effect has
separated from warlord-divided former Somalia, thus imitating the
Eritrea example, by reproducing the old (British and Italian) colonial boundaries. Groups in Zanzibar have inspired counterpart
groups on mainland Tanzania in advocating separation. Other regional resistance groups, ethnically linked, sputter in Casamance
(Senegal), in Chad, and in Niger. After more than 20 years of spo-
radic civil war, Sudan has yet to find a mutually acceptable framework for resolving the cultural-religious differences between north
and south (Malwal 1990).

Secession, partition, and confederation resolve the problem of
ethnic minorities by regional fragments. Smaller minority groups

in conflict with larger neighbors are better served by stronger central governments, but only in a democratic context. The Nigerian example of multiplying regions to reflect local differences obviously has limits. If indeed peaceful partitions can be contemplated, then the security and economic advantages of loose territorial confederations can grow more palpable, especially as pluralized political authorities become more acceptable. (For example, Swaziland and Lesotho may come to be even more closely attached to South Africa.) So functional federalism (divided power within states) finds a parallel in territorial confederations of states.

A concern for constitutional engineering reverses the implications of the preconditions-of-democracy thesis (Lipset 1960; Almond and Verba 1963). Democratic institutions may cause, rather than result from, a civic culture or a democratic personality. Democratization is served not by "trust and tolerance," but rather by "very uncivic behavior such as warfare and internal social conflict" (Lemarchand 1992: 101). Island Mauritius (connected to, if not exactly in, Africa) is perhaps the examplar functioning democracy in a clearly divided communal society. It has found its success by constitutional engineering, with devices for compensating losers in the spirit of consociationalism (Brautigam 1995). Rather than a barrier to the establishment of democratic government, ethnic conflict may be seen as a companion in the process of solving the problems along the way (Ottaway 1995).

### The Tide of Democratic Elections

While the record of African multiparty systems in coping with ethnic conflict in the past is not auspicious, there is illumination in Hayward's distinction between the actual voting process and the rules for mobilization for electoral competition: Elections "provide a vehicle for the expression of both formal and nonformal opposition, and may even have the effect of reducing tensions and accommodating opposition. . . . The problem is not in elections per se, but rather in the politicization and mobilization of ethnicity" (1987: 275, 281). Based on his governmental experience in Ghana, the economist W. Arthur Lewis prefigured Hayward's work, endorsing the consent-seeking, participation function of elections in West African states, while counseling that the choosing-deciding role of elections must avoid exclusionist results (1965: 72–73). But there are tensions between the decision function of democratic elections and conflict regulation that depend on the acceptance of the results. A constitutionalist solution is to limit the decisiveness of the electoral process by power-sharing institutions and by electoral mechanics that produce representation of a wide range of opinion and interests in the results (Lijphart 1977, 1984).

The decline of authoritarianism in Africa, the upsurge of political liberalization, and multiparty elections characterize the first half of the decade of the 1990s. Multipartyism has been instituted in virtually all sub-Saharan African states. Despite a thin and restricted democratic culture and much foreign pressure to institute competitive elections, the disillusionment with authoritarian rule and the urge toward a more accountable leadership is widespread. A measure of the broad gauge of support among a great variety of groups can be gained from the rapid emergence of national conferences in six francophone states in 1990 and 1991 and their equivalents—constitution-making assemblies—in Namibia, South Africa, and Ethiopia (Robinson 1994: 575–577).

In 1990 alone, twenty-one African governments initiated reforms opening the political process to democratic measures. Eleven authoritarian incumbent leaders were ousted via multiparty elections in 1990 to 1994. In five additional elections in the same period incumbents won, but elements of political liberalization were retained (Mutua 1992; Joseph 1991; Robinson 1994; Ndulu and van de Walle 1996: 29). It appears that five years of elections—for presidencies, for national assemblies, for local and provincial councils—are establishing a measure of competitiveness despite the advantages of incumbency and controversies over degrees of "free and fair." (Clark 1997; Vengroff 1993, 1994; Villalon 1994; Oquaye 1995; Chikulo 1996).

The dynamics of a democratization process would have predicted that competitive processes would create opportunities for the stridency of ethnic claims, by way of expanded popular expectations and through the adversarial and uncontrolled nature of the electoral process (Brass 1985; Horowitz 1985; Olorunsola 1986; Diamond 1987). Perhaps the view of the first years of post-authoritarianism was optimistic. Early observations discerned "how broad-based and transethnic are the movements opposing" authoritarian regimes (Joseph 1991: 20). Other contemporaneous commentary observed either nonethnic voting or transethnic coalitions occurring, in Zambia (Bratton 1992), in Kenya (Gerkie 1993), and in Nigeria (Oyediran and Agbaje 1991). Still others pointed to the continual evidence of tribal voting "along predictable ethnic lines, underscoring the continued relevance of subnationalism three decades into statehood" (Decalo 1992: 31). The "evidence shows that democracy is generally perceived as a zero-sum game with definite winners and losers among a country's ethnoregional communities" (Lemarchand 1992: 104).

Over more than 35 years, the record of elections in Africa is a discontinuous one. There is no steady development of experience with rules and forms that could be evaluated and adjusted. The terminal stages of colonialism exhibited not only majoritarian electoral systems but also a variety of consensus-type systems: multistage balloting, reserved seats for groups, and special electoral rolls (Collier 1982: 36–43). In the March 1957 election in Kenya, plurality voting in geographic constituencies was called into question—voters could qualify for up to three votes (Engholm 1960: 406–407, 457–458). The object at that time was to restrict the power of the African masses and favor minorities valued by the colonial regime: white settlers, Asians, chiefs, professionals. Along with pre-independence federations, these "fancy franchises" were perceived as a continuation of an old policy of divide and rule and as delaying tactics on the path to territorial independence. African anticolonial nationalists disparaged the attention paid to political development or institutional transfer as "constitution-mongering" (Price 1960: 165).

Ethnic issues were paramount from the start of independence and even before, but nationalists branded displays of ethnic allegiance as subversive, and as a result they ignored or distorted legitimate constitutional questions that reflected problems of ethnopolitics. Africans were joined by populist democrats elsewhere in emphasizing the need for an activist government and for social-ist-style planning. Nevertheless, while overt manifestations of trib-alism were banned, "hegemonical exchange" characterized "state-facilitated coordination" of "ethno-regional [and other] interests" (Rothchild 1985: 73).

### Vertical Federalism: Elections and Ethnopolitics

The expansion of political space in the democratization 1990s in African states has spawned constitutional changes characteristic of democratic systems elsewhere, with the aim (at least on paper) of achieving legislative and executive accountability, protection of rights and division of governmental functions and even powers. In some cases, such as Ethiopia, South Africa, Namibia, Mali, and Ghana, new constitutions have been drafted, and in other cases, such as Kenya, Tanzania, and Zambia, they have been amended to accom-modate more open politics and multiparty systems. While paper guarantees must be fully activated, they stand as beacons of ap-peal. Struggles to exercise rights lead to pluralizing and diffusing the effects of government; they contribute to "vertical federalism."

Still in the embryonic stage in African states, these efforts include dividing functions and powers at the center, such as establishing more independent roles for legislatures in relation to the executive (a current struggle in Namibia and Tanzania), creating more au-tonomous judiciaries and election commissions in relation to cen-tral governments, providing for two-chamber parliaments (South Africa), or establishing independent central banks (in effect for francophone Africa and a repeated recommendation of international financial instituitions). Elections for national executive, national as-semblies, and local councils function as additional mechanisms to-ward vertical federalism. They complement efforts in horizontal (ter-ritorial) federalism such as those in Ethiopia and South Africa.

### Election Rules

As illustrated in the preceding chapter, elections are highly ma-nipulable and can affect conflict management efforts. Remarks here are confined to issues of ethnic representation. Elections can be structured so they reduce chances of exclusionism. There has now been considerable straying from colonial inheritances in decision rules for electoral choice in African states. An earlier generation of social scientists warned that there was a "case here for the introduction of multimember constituencies with some sort of proportional representation by voting for party lists" (W. J. M. Mackenzie, commenting on ethnoregional party hegemonies in Nigerian elections in 1957 [1960: 473]). Mackenzie (1960: 32–35) also tolerated temporary and limited communal electoral rolls in introducing free elections in divided societies, although he feared cementing divisions among communities. He recognized the occasional necessity for reserved seats, while preferring constituencies geographically drawn to guarantee minority representation. W. Arthur Lewis (1965: 72–73) favored proportional representation in a few large multimember districts. He believed it would reduce regional—and hence ethnic or religious—conflict and produce adequate representation for minorities, thus discouraging parochialism. He favored the single transferable vote over the party list, in order to reduce control by party bosses.

### Elections and Minority Exclusion

The evidence of the strength of ethnicity in election dynamics and results is mixed, despite the tendency of recent competitive elections to evoke ethnopolitics. The process tends to stimulate incumbent and opposition parties to depend primarily on the support of "their" ethnic groups, but not everywhere. Inspection of the voting patterns does not show ethnic parties forming at every opportunity. Both winning and losing parties in several places show signs of transethnic appeal. While we do not see stable patterns of interethnic and multiethnic governing coalitions and opposition coalitions, neither are such vectors completely absent. Mauritius has been governed in a stable fashion with cross-communal coalition parties. (Brautigam [1995] also suggests the absence of an internal threat from the military.)

Patterns of ethnic splits based on personal followings, as well as ethnic party competition, can be discerned in the presidential and parliamentary elections in a number of states since 1990 (Glickman

1995: passim). In the Ghanaian presidential and legislative elections of 1992, there was strong support among the Ewe for Jerry Rawlings and the victorious Provisional National Defense Council (PNDC) and among the Ashanti for Albert Adu Boahen and the defeated New Patriotic Party (NPP), but there was also considerable transethnic support for both parties (Oquaye 1995: 270–272). Mali in 1992 allowed regional and ethnic parties, but the major contests in presidential and national assembly elections were among transethnic parties (Vengroff 1993, 1994). Senegal's "semi-democratic" system has continued transethnic party competition in a series of elections (Young and Kante 1992; Vengroff and Creevey 1997: 215–218; Villalon 1994: 192–193). In Niger, characterized as exhibiting a recent period of "inane partisanship," ethnic parties and ethnic competition within parties were less important than personal followings, and, finally, the corporate influence of the military. In Benin, the national conference in 1990 declared ethnicity and regionalism off limits, but instituted quotas for seats for a variety of groups and worked through consensus procedures. The major parties drew the bulk of their support from major ethnic groups in elections since 1991, yet succeeded in alliance formation and have peacefully returned the former military dictator-turned-civilian politician, who lost the election after the national conference that turned him out (Decalo 1997: 53–60).

In Congo-Brazzaville, ethnic party competition, reflecting long-standing regional differences, led to violence in 1993–94 (Clark 1997). In Kenya, ethnic politics has been the object of much academic and journalistic scrutiny. There the Moi-Kenya African National Union (KANU) government instigated a campaign of ethnic cleansing of "foreigners" in the Kalenjin region before the 1992 presidential and parliamentary elections. The government depended on Kalenjin support to win, although it drew support from twenty-one ethnic groups. It was mightily helped by personal conflicts among opposition leaders, which split the Kikuyu and separated the Luo from a previous alliance with one Kikuyu element. Pragmatism, leading to cooperation among the opposition parties, would have defeated the incumbents in both sets of elections.

In Côte d'Ivoire, transethnic cooperation continues, although the ethnic theme is a recessive element in the politics of personal followings and antiforeignism (Widner 1991: 36; Mundt 1997: 191–198). In the case of Ethiopia, in which a guerrilla war defeated ethnic authoritarianism, the Oromo Liberation Front (OLF) boycotted the subsequent election, charging Tigrayan domination of the newly inaugurated, confederal, ethnoregional government (Rock 1996: 96–97). In Zambia, there is little open campaigning on the basis of ethnic politics; an interesting post-election phenomenon is maintaining the initial landslide: an inclusive coalition that overthrows authoritarian rule, as occurred in Zambia, that lasts too long (Horowitz 1993; Ihonvbere 1994b). The victorious Movement for Multiparty Democracy (MMD) may have been too inclusive, in that previously excluded groups could not share in the rewards of victory proportionate to their perceived deprivation, thus leading to splinter opposition parties that reflect disappointments cast occasionally in terms of ethnic groups. But the rivalry between the United National Independence Party (UNIP) and its replacement MMD (after two elections) is largely between Kenneth Kaunda and Frederick Chiluba (Chikulo 1996; Bratton 1995; van de Walle 1995).

Botswana, which has had competitive elections since independence, could be described as a durable democracy. Observers note that subnationality, ethnic-clan identification explains three-fourths of the vote in previous elections, with both the governing party and the opposition transethnic in their political outreach (Holm 1989; Charlton 1993: 353–363). Competitive elections in multiethnic societies remain vulnerable to ethnic party outbidding, but the record of elections under differing systems of decision choice produce no uniform trend toward inexorably deepening ethnic divisions or ethnic violence.

The most difficult case for moderating ethnic conflict is when competitive elections replace hegemonic rulers in a "bifurcated regime." In Burundi and Rwanda, elections reproduced the divisions apparent in the previous military regimes, despite the efforts of elected presidents to reach out to the elements of the disaffected minority (Longman 1997: 289–293). North-south ethnoregional divisions are being manipulated by political leaders in Togo and Congo-Brazzaville (Heilbrunn 1997; Clark 1997).

In institutional experimentation dealing with the issue of minority exclusion, Nigeria and South Africa stand out. Both have employed mechanisms for minority group inclusion. South Africa has installed a proportional representation electoral system in elections to national and provincial assemblies (Johnston 1994; Reynolds 1994: 184–186). South Africa's transitional constitution reflected strategies of consociationalism, combining federalism with PR voting (Ellmann 1994: 5–44; Reynolds 1995b: 89–98; Sisk 1995a). The National Party, largely representing whites, and the Inkatha Freedom Party, representing a considerable segment of the Zulu ethnoregional minority, shared executive responsibility in the transitional Government of National Unity in cabinet appointments, in representation in seats in the national and provincial assemblies, and in local government.

Opinion remains divided on constitutional engineering toward democracy. Some African observers, presumably close to the scene, seem least satisfied with it. Efforts in Nigeria, where regional and ethnic divisions have dominated politics, and where there have been three tumultuous eras of elections, have produced commentary ranging from lukewarm to negative (Nnoli 1980; Ake 1991; Olorunsola 1986; Oyediran and Agbaje 1991). Other Africans and outsiders display various degrees of confidence in engineering arrangements that reflect pluralism (Horowitz 1993; Ekeh 1990; Ravenhill 1988; Zimmerman 1994).

Nigerian politics has been poisoned by corruption and military autocracy, but between scandals, coups, and human rights abuses, considerable thought and consultation produced the design of lamentably short-lived civilian regimes in order to diffuse ethnic tensions, and especially to reduce minority ethnic groups' perceptions of exclusion. Nigeria's constitutions attempted to diminish ethnoregional divisions and "tribal parties" in ways that encouraged the distribution of ethnic group satisfactions and cross-ethnic support for parties and political candidates (Dent 1995; Nnoma 1995: 313–331; Diamond 1983, 1987, 1991a). The multiplication of states from 1967 onward extended federalism to break the regional power of the three major ethnonationalities and their territorial party manifestations. The "federal character" principle of the 1979 constitution was meant to have major institutions, such as parties, the cabinet, federal commissions, and the formula for electing the president, reflect the diversity of the states, which in turn would manifest an ethnic group balance for the whole country (Ayoade 1986).

Changing the relationship between votes and representation by using proportional representation voting was not tried in Nigeria. Yet authorizing only two territorial parties necessitates coalition making, in this case after candidate nomination primaries and before elections, rather than after the elections—as in PR tied to parliamentary government. The 1992 senate and assembly elections and the last, ill-fated presidential election in 1993 in Nigeria were contested by the mandated two parties, under a ban on ethnic or regional parties, and with plurality voting in geographic constituencies. (Ironically, before the military annulled the results, victory apparently had gone to the presidential candidate who headed a balanced ticket with appeal beyond his home region.)

### Elections and Civic Representation

The nearest approach to a new analytical paradigm is the interest in the growth of a civil society as a basis for democratization. Liberalizing political systems also creates space for civil society. National elections recruit participants, legitimize decisions, and represent partisan groups, but they do not foreclose other means of civic representation and participation by claimant groups. One aspect of ethnic associations enhances the interests of ordinary people against a predatory state and toward self-reliance in the economy. On the other hand, an increase in strength of functional groupings and associations, with judicious infusions of organizational expertise and money from the outside, aids in the process of interest development, and makes for modest cross-cutting cleavages in relation to ethnic affiliations in urban areas. The same enlargement of politics that permits the coagulation of ethnic identities also permits a richer associational life and thus enhancement of opportunity for access to and pressure on government through such routes as church, trade union, profession, or producer co-operative.

Multiplying elective offices and differentiating the scope of their authority give minorities several chances to affect policies, reducing loser-lose-everything anxieties. Not all elections need to directly connect individual citizens to government. Elections for group-based or geographically based second chambers can have the same effect as indirect elections in providing alternative representation for ethnic groups vulnerable to permanent minority status in democratric elections. Traditional chieftainship never disappeared as a parallel recessive line of authority to public government in African states. Its institutional revival in second chambers at the national and provincial levels in constitutional democratic states bears further exploration. The capacity of these functionally federalist devices needs strengthening. They help process and channel demands and reduce the burden of direct constituency pressure on policymaking (Ndulu and van de Walle 1996: 22).

Elections that initially serve as an ethnic census need not be destructive if the election rules provide for progressively fair competition. Mackenzie (1960: 103–106) made independent election commissions and judges the basis for the inauguration of free elections. Too many African election commissions and the rules they made in the 1990s converted them into arms of the incumbent government or the incumbent presidential candidate. In addition, rules for voting choice that reduce the vote-seat disproportionality encourage minority representation. Yet elections are only one of the tools of constitutional democracy. Elections authorize a certain distribution of power, but there are numerous other ways that interests and identities can be represented, as in the politics of functional federalism: divided power and a pluralistic civil society.

The timing of elections in the process of constitutionalizing a transition from authoritarianism may be critical. Testing support for newly emergent democratic parties argues for an early "founding" election. Such early elections can be destabilizing. On the other hand, the making of pacts and the establishing of rules of competition argue for an election at a later moment in the transition, because the yield is more time for educating the population on the terms of acceptance, despite the tactical desires of the negotiators (Mattes 1994: 3–8; Harrison 1996: 30–35; Zartman 1995: 270).

The national conference phenomenon, exemplified in Benin, and the series of agreements, "minutes," the Convention for a Democratic South Africa (CODESA), and other negotiations characterizing the transition in South Africa, both suggest that a considerable period of discussion before actual elections reduces the destabilizing potential of ethnic divisions (Robinson 1995; Decalo 1997; Frost 1996; Sisk 1995a). Power-sharing results of elections, if they contribute to policy debates among groups, including ethnopolitical groups, can develop into "continuing negotiating forums." They serve as the equivalent of national conferences to achieve consensus on major issues (Ottaway 1995). While all this may postpone individualist democracy, it can buy time for building the capacity of governmental institutions.

## Horizontal (Territorial) Federalism and Ethnopolitics

Elections in multiregional (horizontal) federal systems, which retain elements of central control, lead to outcomes for ethnoregional parties that yield mixed stakes in the overall system (Munroe 1994: 677–682). Territorial federalism modifies the effects of the perceived threat of exclusion, by counteracting the tendency of a regional majority/national minority to dominate governments of unified powers (Lewis 1965: 49–55; Smith 1995: 9–10). Staggering national, provincial, and local elections in territorial federations buys time for bargaining upward in cases of small minorities and creates opportunities for cross-cutting pressures to operate on larger minorities or majority ethnic parties. On the other hand, territorial federalism risks the entrenchment of recalcitrant minorities in regional enclaves, threatens to dissatisfy new subminorities seeking institutional expression of emerging group identities, invites struggle over control of resources, especially taxing powers, and, at the extreme, can create constant concern over secession (Agnew 1995: 297–300).

As a result of the global attention paid to South Africa, the modest federalist provisions of the final constitution may acquire more influence elsewhere in Africa. Thus far, only elements in the political leadership of KwaZulu/Natal have pressed for more provincial powers. A white "boerstaat" within the country remains a possibility.

Divisions in Sudan and in the Somalilands, and the present troubles in erstwhile Zaire (now the Democratic Republic of Congo, in which Shaba and the Kasais have been virtually autonomous for several years), may cause more serious consideration of territorial confederal arrangements as part of final settlements. The Ethiopian experiment will be watched carefully in Zanzibar, Sudan, and Congo. The path to territorial federalist settlements may become more acceptable if supplemented by consociational arrangements (Agnew 1995: 300). New large-scale horizontal federal arrangements, based on entirely redrawn and more ethnically representative borders or ultra-localized communitarian governments, cannot be ruled out (Laurent and Paquet 1991).

A territorial federalism that countenances ethnopolitics also counteracts it by prescribing provincial boundaries in sufficient number to cut across previously strong expressions of ethnoregionalism. Positive contribution to rewards for interethnic moderation can come from federalism that maintains a stake in a strong central government, so that regionally strong ethnic parties can find coalition partners at the level of central government. (A mandated two-party system performs the same function). The temporary constitutional compromise in South Africa that preceded the election of April 1994 resulted in Inkatha and the Nationalists, junior partners in the national governing coalition, each winning at the subnational provincial level. The great object of federalism—horizontal or vertical—is to contribute to the achievement of a dual citizenship, that of a region and that of the nation—a cultural identity as well as a territorial citizenship (Sklar 1993: 87–98; Ekeh 1975, 1990).

## Conclusion

Ethnic conflict is not Africa's only problem. Other powerful, debilitating forces are at work. Weak and debt-ridden economies of low or zero growth, the increasing gap between the well-off and the poor, the spreading normality of graft and corruption, the continuing strength of the military, and the widespread availability of small arms also undermine the urgency and continuing support of

a government by popular consent. Some sort of elected governments likely will survive in many post-authoritarian African states,
not least because they channel domestic pressure and satisfy international standards. Naked authoritarianism pays a higher price for
survival than it did ten years ago.

Nevertheless, ethnic and regional pluralism will have to be reflected in the practices of competitively elected governments. This
is a pattern that has been recognized in the politics of all African
states for many years. It seems clear that participation by ethnic
groups and ethnic parties in democratized politics will not be eliminated, and it will be suppressed only by undermining democracy.
Ethnic loyalty continues to play a positive role for many people,
offering security, reciprocity, and protection of interests in an environment of vulnerability. The sense that ethnic communities are
in political competition will not go away, and it is behind the
formation of parties as politics is liberalized. In most African states,
the problem persists of the great gap between the proximate rewards of winning office, thus controlling public resources and not.
There is low incentive for sharing and high reward for not sharing
when public office is the only game in town. Africa needs a larger
private sector as an arena for rewards and achievement.

If the private sector is to grow, Africa needs stronger civilian
political institutions to guarantee enterprise and attract investment.
It has been argued that democracy is less important than building
strong institutions—public and civic—that support economic development (van de Walle 1995: 128–141; Gyimah-Boadi and van
de Walle 1996: 221–226). Developmental states require strong links
between state and society, through an effective bureaucracy and a
sense of common purpose. As summarized by van de Walle, the
fate of Africa's new democracies therefore depend on "enhancing
administrative capacity, . . . promoting the rule of law, . . . establishing agencies of restraint, . . . forging policy consensus" (1995:
136–139). Constitutional democracy provides for restraining popular will as well as central power, not only through achieving balanced government but by restricting the reach of government. A
constitutional democracy that respects liberty balances bureaucratic
and democratic systems of authority (Cohen 1996: 49–51). Central

banks, courts, and business corporations need to operate in some important respects outside the political democracy of citizenship equality, the current situation characteristic of the older existing democratic governments today. The strengthening of such institutions also provides for arenas of representation and success outside the central government for expressions of group identity. Constitutional engineering to include consensus electoral systems by reducing ethnic group insecurity will contribute to a new sense of commonality to make the economic sacrifices required for economic growth. With growth comes further social complexity, which over the long run tends to weaken localism.

Strengthening the rule of law also connotes the demilitarization of society, perhaps the most important issue governing the fate of democracy in Africa today. The costs to business and civil liberties of the depredations of "police, militia, customs, and army units . . . should not be underestimated" (van de Walle 1995:137). Equally significant is the drag exerted on potential foreign investment and on continuing flows of public funds by the threat of military intervention by oversized armed forces. A downsized military and police, disciplined and under civilian control, is fundamental for constitutional engineering to do its work.[1]

# ■ PART II: Electoral Systems

If constitutional engineering is a critically important lever for promoting peace in deeply divided multiethnic societies, and electoral systems are especially important, then the specifics of various electoral systems deserve careful attention. The three essays that follow debate the appropriateness of various electoral systems for meaningful representation and for managing conflict (especially ethnic conflict) in Africa. The debate distinguishes advocates of single-member-district, majoritarian systems, such as Barkan (chapter 3), from those who advocate proportional representation, such as Reynolds (chapter 4).

Mozaffar, in chapter 5, then applies his analysis of the electoral system debate directly to the issues stimulated by the essays in part I. He argues for a more qualified understanding of the role of constitutional engineering to promote democratization and conflict management, emphasizing the need to understand the underlying political calculus behind the choices that parties make to choose one system over another.

# 3

# RETHINKING THE APPLICABILITY OF PROPORTIONAL REPRESENTATION FOR AFRICA

Joel D. Barkan

The successful transitions to democracy in Namibia and South Africa have renewed claims by advocates of proportional representation (PR) that it is the most appropriate electoral formula for the rest of Africa and other plural societies. Their argument, as articulated by Andrew Reynolds and Arend Lijphart, contains four essential elements (Reynolds 1995a; Lijphart 1985, 1994). First, they argue that PR is the "fairest" method for electing members of national legislatures. Second, they say that PR is inclusive because it ensures that all significant players in the political system, including potential spoilers, are represented in the legislature. PR thus enhances the prospects that all players will support the constitutional order by participating in its elections and principal institutions. Such support is particularly important during the early stages of new or recently restored democratic rule, when the institutionalization of the new constitutional order is incomplete. Their third argument is that PR facilitates arrangements of power sharing or consociational democracy, enabling most political forces to have a voice in the governance of the political system. Fourth—and this last benefit results from the first three—PR greatly raises the prospects for democratization in plural societies where political cleavages run deep and mirror ethnic, racial, linguistic, or religious divisions.

Although the recent experience in Southern Africa appears to support the argument for PR, the advantages of this system—particularly for the rest of the continent and other similar societies—are not as clear-cut as they seem. In agrarian societies, in which the overwhelming majority of the people derive their livelihood from the land, PR often does not produce electoral results that are significantly fairer or more inclusive than plurality or majoritarian elections based on single member districts (SMDs). PR is not, therefore, an essential requisite for consociational government, but rather one method for facilitating power sharing within the executive branch.

PR also has serious disadvantages, one of which should be of particular concern to any would-be constitutional engineer for an agrarian society. Because under the purest forms of PR, legislative seats are allocated from party lists according to each party's proportion of the total national vote, individual members of parliament (MPs) do not identify with, nor can they be held accountable to, the residents of a specific geographic constituency. Yet in agrarian societies, this lack of linkage between elected representatives and constituents greatly reduces the prospects for the long-term consolidation of democratic rule.

## Representation in Agrarian Societies

In agrarian societies, where the level of occupational specialization and class identity is low, most people differentiate themselves from each other and define their interests in terms of where they live, rather than on the basis of what they do. This is particularly true in Africa, where 50 to 90 percent of the population are peasants. They have a high attachment to the place where they reside and affection for their neighbors. Their approach to elections is to focus on the basic needs of their local community and surrounding region—whether they have adequate water, schools, and health-care facilities, whether there is a farm-to-market road, whether the producer price for the agricultural commodity grown in their area yields a fair return to local farmers. Inhabitants of the same rural areas usually have a common set of political interests, and they vote accordingly. This explains why a distinguishing feature of recent multiparty elections in Africa is the high geographic concentration of the vote for competing parties. Except in urban areas, whose inhabitants come from many different regions and tend to have a relatively strong sense of occupational and class identity, people who live in the same place vote for the same political party.[1] In agrarian societies, people evaluate both parties and candidates in terms of their potential for, or past record of, constituency service (Barkan 1984).

Yet PR systematically frustrates the fulfillment of such voter expectations. Not only are MPs not responsible for addressing the needs of specific localities, but their political careers depend primarily on satisfying the expectations of their party's leadership, which determines their rankings on the party's list for the next election. In agrarian societies, and particularly in Africa, the use of PR risks the emergence of what Goran Hyden (1981: 7) has termed "the suspended state"—a state that is disconnected from the population, and that eventually loses its authority and its ability to govern.

Democratization depends on the simultaneous existence of two different relationships—(1) *representation* of citizens by their chosen leaders, a relationship characterized by dialogue and accountability, and (2) *tolerance, bargaining, and compromise* among rival political groups. The first links elites and nonelites who have a common political interest, and constitutes the "vertical" dimension of democracy. The second obtains mainly between leaders of opposing interests, and constitutes the "horizontal" dimension of democracy.

The relative importance of these two dimensions is different during transitions to democracy and during democratic consolidation. Because transitions involve the establishment of a new constitutional order that must be embraced by all significant factions, they are marked by intense bargaining between rival elites. At this stage, relatively little emphasis is placed on the quality of representation. It is more or less taken for granted that key elites are bargaining on behalf of their respective constituencies. For example, during the negotiations over South Africa's transition to democracy, few questioned whether Nelson Mandela and Cyril Ramaphosa, on the one hand, or F.W. de Klerk and Roelf Meyer, on the other, spoke for the rank and file of the African National Congress and the National Party, respectively.

Consolidation, on the other hand, is a long-term process during which democratic practice is gradually institutionalized. Indeed, it can be said that the process of consolidation never ceases, because for democracy to survive, successive generations of citizens and elites must reaffirm their nation's commitment to it.[2] Hence, consolidation requires the *continuous* fulfillment of both the vertical and horizontal dimensions of democracy, and any electoral formula that does not sustain both undermines the prospects for democracy over the long term. Judged by these criteria, the advantages and disadvantages of PR are clear. While it can facilitate transitions to democracy in plural societies, when these societies are also agrarian, it impedes consolidation by failing to sustain democracy's vertical component.

### Second Thoughts About PR in Southern Africa

The experience of Southern Africa provides substantial evidence of PR's primary shortcoming, and has given rise to calls for the system's abolition or modification. PR was used in Namibia for that country's first all-race elections in November 1989. The elections were held to establish a constituent assembly that subsequently became the National Assembly (or lower house of parliament) after Namibia's independence in March 1990. Seventy-two seats were allocated on the basis of the total nationwide vote of the contesting parties—that is, the party vote in a single national constituency. The same variation of PR was used for Namibia's second parliamentary elections in December 1994. In between, Namibians elected thirteen regional councils in November 1992 from ninety-five single member districts. Each council in turn elected two of its members to the upper house of parliament, the National Council. The outcomes are instructive.

The South West Africa People's Organisation (SWAPO) obtained majorities of 57.3 and 77.7 percent in the first two parliamentary elections, and has governed since independence. The principal op-position party, the Democratic Turnhalle Alliance (DTA), obtained 28.6 percent of the vote in 1989 and 20.8 percent in 1994, and the United Democratic Front (UDF) obtained 5.6 and 2.7 percent. The use of PR resulted in an allocation of seats to each party that closely approximated each party's percentage of the vote.

With more than two-thirds of the seats in the National Assembly, SWAPO has the power to amend Namibia's constitution. Thus, PR by itself has failed to provide sufficient minority representation to block constitutional changes that could be injurious to minority interests. Nor has PR guaranteed the inclusion of minority representatives in the executive branch—the essence of consociational democracy. Rather, it is the self-restraint of the majority government of President Sam Nujoma, along with international pressure, that has been responsible for the protection of minority interests—particularly the property rights of Namibia's white population.[3] Self-restraint and commitment to a policy of national reconciliation have also resulted in the appointment of several members of opposition parties to minor posts in the government and to the position of attorney general.

Most significantly, Namibia's ethnic and racial minorities, which supported the DTA and the UDF, would be no worse off and possibly would be better off with an electoral system based on SMDs. Because the vote in the 1994 parliamentary elections was tabulated and reported by the ninety-five constituencies that elect the regional councils, it is possible to estimate the distribution of seats that would have occurred had the elections been run under an SMD formula. The results show SWAPO obtaining a plurality or majority of the vote in 66.7 percent of the ninety-five districts, the DTA obtaining a plurality or majority in 29.7 percent, and the UDF in 3.1 percent.[4] *The distribution of seats is thus substantially the same under the two systems.* Advocates of PR claim that SMD overrepresents parties that obtain a plurality or a majority of the vote; yet the Namibian case shows that it can also underrepresent the majority party, and thus may provide better protection of minority interests than PR. For example, the DTA—the party of Namibia's white community and ethnic minorities—obtained only 20.8 percent of the votes in the 1994 election, but would have "won" 29.5 percent of the seats had each councilmanic district elected a representative to the National Assembly. Moreover, SMD systems can be fine-tuned so as to reduce (or maintain) the associated disparity between vote shares and seats won, as explained below.

The Namibian case also demonstrates the failure of PR to provide appropriate representation for the residents of agrarian societies. Interviews that two colleagues and I conducted with more than three dozen regional councilors in July 1994 consistently revealed that members of the National Assembly rarely make an appearance in the rural areas, because they have no constituency to which they are accountable. By contrast, the regional councilors—precisely because they are elected from geographically defined constituencies and are physically accessible within their districts—are the elected officials to whom citizens bring their problems and those of their communities (Barkan, Bauer, and Martin 1994). This is hardly surprising. In agrarian societies, in which most residents are peasant farmers who move about on foot, by bicycle, or by public transportation, the most effective representation occurs on a face-to-face basis in the countryside or rural towns.

It also is not surprising that this difference in the quality of representation between PR and district-based systems is becoming a political issue in Namibia and within SWAPO. Because of the failure of PR to facilitate a continuous dialogue between MPs and the rural population, regional councilors want an end to PR for elections to the National Assembly, as well as a devolution of power to the regional councils. Some also believe that a change to an SMD system would enable them to challenge incumbent MPs at the next parliamentary election. For the same reasons, incumbent MPs and the SWAPO leadership oppose a change of electoral system. The disagreement over electoral approach also reflects a "generation gap": councilors tend to be five to ten years younger than MPs. The issue is likely to build by the time of the next elections in 1999. Indeed, the SWAPO government recently announced that the next local government elections in Namibia will be conducted through PR and party lists rather than the current system of ward representation, a decision that has both surprised and alarmed those already critical of the use of PR at the national level (Bauer, forthcoming).

The failure of PR to provide adequate representation of local interests has resulted in similar calls for district-based voting in South Africa. As in Namibia, the demand for changing the electoral system has come mainly from politicians who are most concerned about how the African National Congress (ANC) can better represent and strengthen its ties to the grassroots of South African society—politicians who tend to be younger or who view themselves as representatives of local constituencies. Conversely, the staunchest defenders of PR are the leaders of the ruling party, including President Mandela, who are more concerned with fostering national unity among South Africa's racial and ethnic communities and with maintaining their control over subordinate leaders within the ANC.

South Africa elects the members of its National Assembly through a "two tier" version of PR: 200 seats of the Assembly are allocated among contesting parties on the basis of their total national vote using a Droop quota system, and 200 are allocated on the same basis in each of nine regions.[5] In the first all-race election, held in April 1994, this application of PR resulted in each party obtaining a proportion of seats that was virtually identical to its percentage of the total vote. Under South Africa's interim constitution, parties winning at least twenty seats are guaranteed participation in the government proportionate to their vote, a provision for power sharing that will end after the next general election in 1999.[6]

Notwithstanding the virtues of "fairness" and "inclusion," the absence of a representational link between individual MPs and specific geographic constituencies has been apparent from the start. Leaders of local civic organizations are unsure of how to obtain representation or assistance for their communities when there is no MP accountable to them. Few MPs make systematic efforts to identify and respond to the concerns of particular local areas other than those with which they have prior association, because they do not know how or where to begin. Recognizing the downsides of this situation, the ANC announced in October 1994 that it was establishing an informal system of constituency-based representation by assigning MPs and cabinet ministers to a series of designated areas, and by providing each MP with R3,000 (about $890) per month to maintain a presence in these areas.[7]

It is unlikely that this one incentive will overcome the many disincentives present when a party-list-based system of electoral representation is employed in a young democracy where most legislators are serving for the first time: many MPs live great distances from the quasi-districts to which they have been assigned, a situation compounded by the fact that a disproportionate number reside in the area in and around Johannesburg. Few have the requisite skills or field staff necessary to establish an effective presence in the constituency.[8] Virtually none maintains a constituency field office, although some have established field offices on a joint basis.

Many MPs also seem to be preoccupied with other interests—by the end of 1996 roughly one quarter of the original cohort of ANC members of the National Assembly had left parliament to take up other and more lucrative posts in government or in the private sector.[9] This drain of members is a direct result of PR and the party list system, because the Mandela government is free to transfer elected officials elsewhere—to government ministries including ambassadorial posts, or to other elected bodies (from a regional assembly to the National Assembly or the National Council of the Provinces), and vice versa, simply by replacing them with other individuals on the ANC list. This practice has also been used by National Party leaders to control backbenchers and leaders at the regional level who have been too independent of the center.[10] It is likely to have deleterious effects if continued, and to undermine further the government's attempts to establish institutionalized links between itself and the grassroots of South African society.

Ironically, it was the ANC leadership that long favored a majoritarian electoral system based on single member districts before its negotiations with the National Party that produced the interim constitution under which South Africa is being governed from April 1994 to April 1999. However, ANC leaders changed their position and opted for PR in October 1990 when they concluded that PR was the least offensive method to ensure participation in the first all-race election by the National Party, the Inkatha Freedom Party, and fringe elements such as the Freedom Front that could potentially disrupt the settlement.[11] The fact that public opinion polls showed that the ANC was likely to win an outright majority of the vote, rather than a plurality, also led party leaders to opt for PR. In short, PR was chosen because it facilitated the transition to democratic rule (Sisk 1995b).

PR has not facilitated its consolidation. As noted above, local and regional leaders within the ANC are increasingly frustrated and restive about their inability to hold MPs accountable to their communities. Recent public opinion polls indicate widespread skepticism about the value of parliamentary democracy and the job performance of MPs.[12] These forces resulted in intense discussions within the ANC leadership in 1996 regarding the continued use of PR, and the form of electoral system to be specified in the draft of the new constitution passed by the Constitutional Assembly in May. The lack of consensus among ANC leaders on this issue is apparent from the ambivalent language in the final text: Schedule 3 of the new constitution states that the next general elections, scheduled for April 1999, will be held on the same basis of proportional representation as the elections of 1994. No specification of electoral system is made for subsequent elections[13] as a result of a clear understanding among those who hold opposing views that the issue will be reopened before the elections of 2004. Critical to the resolution of this debate will be an increased appreciation of the fact that the distribution of seats among South Africa's principal parties is likely to be the same under a single member district system of representation as under PR, and that the virtues of both an SMD system and PR can be obtained through a combination of the two, as happened in Germany.

## Similar Results, Different Linkages

Ironically, some of the best evidence for the similarity of the distribution of legislative seats under SMD plurality and PR has been assembled by Andrew Reynolds, a staunch proponent of PR. In a valuable paper in which he "re-runs" the recent elections in South Africa and Malawi, Reynolds shows that the choice of electoral formula is not nearly as significant in agrarian societies as it is in the context of advanced industrial societies (1995c). Reynolds's data, along with my own for the most recent parliamentary elections in Kenya and Namibia, is presented in table 3-1.[14]

Table 3-1 presents the results by political party for four elections in four African countries: South Africa (April 1994), Namibia (December 1994), Malawi (May 1994), and Kenya (December 1992). South Africa's and Namibia's elections were run under PR, and Malawi's and Kenya's were run under SMD plurality. The table allows for comparison of the percentage of seats each party *actually obtained* under the electoral formula used for the election in question with its percentage of the vote, as well a comparison of the percentage of seats actually obtained with the percentage of seats that the party *would have obtained* under alternative electoral formulas.

Thus, the distributions of seats obtained via PR in South Africa and Namibia can be compared with the distributions that would have resulted under plurality SMD, while the distributions of seats obtained via SMD plurality in Malawi and Kenya can be compared with the vote shares obtained by the parties—percentages that would have been approximated by PR. Data for SMD formulas are presented in one or both of two versions—the actual results (as they occurred in Malawi and Kenya) and the estimated results (for South Africa, Namibia, and Kenya) had all districts contained the same number of voters. Finally, the table presents an Index of Disproportionality (ID) (Gallagher 1991) for each formula for which a distribution of seats was calculated, as well as for recent elections in four established democracies that employ plurality SMD. The closer ID is to zero, the closer the electoral formula comes to translating each party's percentage of the vote into exactly the same percentage of seats. Thus, the higher the ID, the greater the disproportionality of the outcome. ID scores typically range from near zero to 20.[15]

Table 3-1 underscores three points. First, except in the case of Kenya, PR and SMD plurality yield substantially the same distribution of seats. Both do (or in the case of Kenya, can do) a good job of translating the percentage of the vote obtained by each party into a similar percentage of seats. Second, PR is the superior method

**Table 3-1.** Distributions of Votes and Seats under PR and SMD Formulas

| | | | % of Seats | | |
|---|---|---|---|---|---|
| Election | Party | % of Vote | National-List PR | Existing SMDs | Equal SMDs* |
| South Africa | ANC | 62.7 | 63.0 | NA | 70.8 |
| (April 1994) | NP | 20.4 | 20.5 | NA | 17.0 |
| | IFP | 10.5 | 10.8 | NA | 12.3 |
| | FF | 2.2 | 2.2 | NA | — |
| | DP | 1.7 | 1.8 | NA | — |
| | PAC | 1.3 | 1.3 | NA | — |
| | ID | | 0.3 | NA | 6.7 |
| Namibia | SWAPO | 73.9 | 73.6 | 67.4 | 73.9 |
| (December 1994) | DTA | 20.8 | 20.8 | 29.5 | 23.9 |
| | UDF | 2.7 | 4.2 | 3.2 | 2.2 |
| | Other | 3.1 | 1.4 | — | — |
| | ID | | 1.1 | 7.7 | 2.2 |
| Malawi | UDF | 46.4 | NA | 48.0 | NA |
| (May 1994) | MCP | 33.7 | NA | 31.6 | NA |
| | AFORD | 18.9 | NA | 20.3 | NA |
| | ID | | NA | 2.1 | NA |
| Kenya | KANU | 29.7 | NA | 53.2 | 44.6 |
| (December 1992) | FORD-A | 24.2 | NA | 16.5 | 22.3 |
| | FORD-K | 20.8 | NA | 16.5 | 17.0 |
| | DP | 22.2 | NA | 12.2 | 15.4 |
| | Other | 3.1 | NA | 1.6 | 0.5 |
| | ID | | NA | 19.1 | 12.0 |
| IDs (average) for selected established democracies with SMD plurality systems: | | | | Canada | 11.3 |
| | | | | N. Zealand | 10.7 |
| | | | | UK | 10.5 |
| | | | | USA | 5.4 |

*Key:* ID, Index of Disproportionality; NA, not available or not applicable; PR, proportional representation; SMD, single-member district.

*Note:* Percentages do not always total 100 due to rounding.

*South Africa:* ANC, African National Congress; DP, Democratic Party; FF, Freedom Front; IFP, Inkatha Freedom Party; NP, National Party; PAC, Pan-Africanist Congress. *Namibia:* DTA, Democratic Turnhalle Alliance; SWAPO, South West Africa People's Organisation; UDF, United Democratic Front. *Malawi:* AFORD, Alliance for Democracy; MCP, Malawi Congress Party; UDF, United Democratic Front. *Kenya:* DP, Democratic Party; FORD-A, Forum for Restoration of Democracy— Asili; FORD-K, Forum for Restoration of Democracy—Kenya; KANU, Kenya African National Union.

*Data for South Africa based on election results as reported in 341 counting districts. Data for Namibia based on election results as reported in 95 councilmanic districts adjusted for population variations among districts. Data for Kenya based on election results in 183 parliamentary constituencies adjusted for population variations among districts. Data for the established democracies from Arend Lijphart, *Electoral Systems and Party Systems* (New York: Oxford University Press, 1994), pp. 160–62.

if achieving a proportional outcome is the sole purpose of an election. However, as argued above, the mere mathematical translation of votes into seats does not guarantee the establishment of a continuous process of representation following the election. When it comes to the quality of representation, SMD plurality is the superior formula. *The question then is whether the benefit of PR's mathematical accuracy is worth the price of flawed representation, or whether the benefit of SMD's superior representation is worth the cost of a small to modest distortion in the translation of votes to seats.*

Third, the deficiencies of plurality SMD formulas are substantially reduced when all districts contain the same number of voters. In Namibia, the average number of voters per district is 5,236, but the number of voters in the existing councilmanic districts varies from 1,051 to 13,592. Here, an SMD system based on districts of equal size would result in an ID nearly as low as the current PR system. The creation of districts with equal numbers of voters would likewise reduce the level of disproportionality in Kenya, where the average number of registered voters per district was 25,544, but numbers varied from 2,872 to 65,887. While the resulting ID is not as low as that for Namibia, the level is near that of several established democracies. Most important, the creation of equal districts in Kenya would reverse the most serious shortcoming of the present SMD system (but one that also "protects" the minority interests of Kenya's smallest and least developed ethnic groups): a legislative majority for a party that obtained barely 30 percent of the vote. Creating more and thus smaller and more compact districts would further reduce the level of disproportionality associated with SMD.

The level of disproportionality depends not so much on the choice of electoral formula as on three other variables: (1) the extent to which voters of different parties are spatially concentrated or dispersed across society, (2) the extent of variation in the number of voters in each district, and (3) the number and compactness of electoral districts. It is for this reason that SMD systems yield (or can be designed to yield) distributions of seats that are close to those obtained through PR.

As explained in the second section of this chapter, voters in agrarian societies tend to vote in geographic blocs that are highly homogeneous in composition. As a result, it is not unusual for parties to obtain high majorities of 70 to more than 90 percent of the vote in some areas and less than 10 or 15 percent in others. What appears from a distance to be a multiparty system is in actuality a collection of regional one-party systems. Malawi and Namibia are near-perfect examples of this tendency, Kenya less so. By contrast, multiparty systems in advanced industrial societies are characterized by a geographic dispersion of the vote. Although different regions are viewed as bastions of different parties, the degree of hegemony is much less than in developing countries, because areas harbor voters from across the political spectrum. Newly industrialized countries fall somewhere in between these two extremes, manifesting a pattern of bloc voting in many rural areas combined with more heterogeneous patterns elsewhere.

The more agrarian the society, then, the higher the geographic concentration of the vote and the more closely the distribution of seats under an SMD system will mirror the distribution of the total vote, as well as the distribution of seats obtained through PR. Conversely, the more industrialized the society, the more geographically dispersed the vote, and the greater the discrepancy between the distribution of legislative seats obtained under SMD and that obtained through PR. In sum, electoral systems based on SMDs are likely to have a low ID in agrarian societies, but moderate to high IDs in industrialized societies.[16] Moreover, the extent of disproportionality associated with SMD systems can be reduced by creating more districts, thus making all districts smaller and more compact. This raises the level of social homogeneity within all districts, and thus increases the extent to which residents support one party or another.

## Conclusions

Because advocates of PR and consociational democracy such as Arend Lijphart have tended to focus their examinations of electoral systems on established democracies and thus on industrial and post-industrial societies, it is not surprising that they have failed to appreciate the extent to which SMD plurality and PR yield similar results in developing countries. Nor, for the same reason, have they been sensitive to the extent to which SMD systems in agrarian societies can be refined to reduce the extent of disproportionality. Finally, advocates of PR have not fully considered the way in which rural voters approach the electoral process. Proponents of PR place a much lower emphasis on the need for geographically based representation, because in societies dominated by interest-group and corporate politics, such representation is no longer required to maintain a democratic constitutional order.

Conceding the need for geographical representation, Andrew Reynolds has argued that a modified application of PR based on multimember districts would overcome its principal defect in agrarian societies. However, if such a system is to facilitate face-to-face contact between citizens and representatives, it would require districts that are so small in size and population as to reduce the number of representatives per district to the point that allocating seats on the principle of proportionality would be either unnecessary or unfeasible. For example, if PR is modified to allocate from three and six seats in each of a series of small multimember districts, why bother? The allocation of such a small number of seats may yield results that are less proportional than SMD plurality. They would certainly be less proportional than ordinary PR.[17]

Advocates of PR and defenders of SMD plurality run the risk of talking past each other. In fact, each formula is particularly appropriate for one subset of political systems, but not necessarily for all. For agrarian societies—especially those of Africa, the world's least developed continent, where the return to democracy is at a critical stage—SMD systems may yet provide an essential ingredient of democracy, without which its consolidation is not likely to occur: effective representation. In this context, any call for the replacement of constituency-based voting with PR is likely to be premature.

# ELECTIONS IN SOUTHERN AFRICA
## The Case for Proportionality, A Rebuttal

Andrew Reynolds

In chapter 3, Joel D. Barkan offers a strong challenge to the newly emerging conventional wisdom that proportional representation is the best electoral formula for the fledgling—and often highly divided—democracies of Africa. First, he criticizes PR for weakening (or even severing) the link between individual MPs and constituents. This hinders the development of the "vertical" dimension of democracy (that is, the representative relationship between elites and nonelites with a common political interest), he says, "greatly reduc[ing] the prospects for the consolidation of democratic rule." For Barkan, the relationship between representative and voter that obtains within a single member district (SMD) best reflects the nature of agrarian societies in Africa, in which the strongest ties are those of kinship, neighborhood, and land, and people "define their [political] interests . . . on the basis of where they live."

While accepting that some degree of proportionality (indicating the protection of minority interests) is a normative good, he argues that the patterns of geographically polarized voting seen in agrarian societies enable SMD plurality systems to produce parliaments that are reasonably reflective of the distribution of the nationwide popular vote. Thus, one of the underpinnings of consociational government (a proportionally constituted parliament) can be retained while the main drawback of PR, the detachment and lack of accountability of representatives elected from party lists, can be avoided.

It is true that when voting patterns closely follow cleavages among groups defined by ascriptive traits (such as race, ethnicity, language, or religion), and when different groups cluster in different areas, elections held under SMD plurality can produce highly proportional results. As Barkan notes, the 1994 general election in Malawi gave rise to a parliament that closely mirrored the distribution of the national vote among the three main parties. An election's Index of Disproportionality (ID) measures the degree to which the distribution of parliamentary seats among parties diverges from the distribution of votes, with zero representing a perfectly proportional outcome. The score on that index for the Malawian election (2.1) was lower than the figures for plurality elections in all but three of the established democracies for which data are presented in Arend Lijphart's comprehensive *Electoral Systems and Party Systems,* which covers the period from 1945 to 1990 (Lijphart 1994). Similarly, the regionally polarized parliamentary election of 1985 in Zimbabwe produced an ID of 2.5, and my own "re-running" of the 1994 parliamentary elections in South Africa and Namibia (which were held under PR systems) indicated that SMD plurality would have produced relatively proportional results, with IDs of 6.7 and 4.0, respectively.[1]

The ID for a given election tells us much about parliamentary composition. High IDs indicate a high likelihood that: (1) minority parties are receiving little or no representation; (2) larger parties are gaining "seat bonuses" over and above their share of the popular vote; (3) governments with 100 percent of the executive power are being catapulted into office with less than 50 percent of the popular vote; and (4) governments based on a simple majority of the popular vote are being awarded supermajority powers (as in South Africa, where the use of a plurality system would have provided the African National Congress, which received 62 percent of the vote, with two-thirds of the seats in the National Assembly— enough to write the new constitution unfettered).

## Atypical Cases

The evidence from Malawi in 1994 and Zimbabwe in 1985 (and the hypothetical evidence from South Africa and Namibia) seems to indicate that, in Southern Africa, SMD plurality can provide the best of both worlds—a proportionally constituted parliament, along with the representational advantages of a district-based system. Barkan claims that "in agrarian societies . . . PR does not produce electoral results that are significantly "fairer" or more inclusive than plurality elections based on SMDs." Yet the results from Malawi and Zimbabwe have not been mirrored in established democracies, in Africa as a whole, or within Southern Africa itself. These are atypical cases, and we must take care not to be blinded by them.

The five countries using SMD plurality for democratic elections in Southern Africa since 1965 have, on average, experienced IDs in line with plurality elections in the rest of the world (table 4-1). The results have been slightly more proportional than those for Africa as a whole but slightly less proportional than those for the established democracies—Britain and the inheritors of its "first-past-the-post" electoral system. Furthermore, the figures for PR elections show that, despite the low IDs for plurality in Malawi and Zimbabwe, when it comes to translating votes into seats, PR is not just marginally superior to SMD plurality, but substantially so. The evidence from throughout Africa suggests that the use of an electoral system based on SMDs does not ensure the proportionality of electoral results. This is true even in agrarian societies, where voting patterns are geographically concentrated. It follows that if proportionality is a necessary feature of consociational democracy, plurality cannot be relied on to secure it.

Even if plurality elections in fledgling democracies produced reasonably proportional results across the board, there would still be worrisome threats to democratic consolidation. First, the experience of South Africa illustrates that the inclusion within parliament of small minority parties can play a crucial stabilizing role in the early years of democratization of a divided society. Clearly, the presence of the Afrikaner Freedom Front (FF), the Pan-Africanist Congress (PAC), and the Democratic Party (DP) in the first nonracial South African parliament has been conducive to an atmosphere of reconciliation. As I noted in "Constitutional Engineering in Southern Africa" (Reynolds 1995b), this measure of political inclusiveness would not have been achieved had the April 1994 elections been run on a plurality system rather than a PR system.

**Table 4-1.** Average IDs of SMD Plurality and PR Elections

|  | Southern Africa | Africa | Established Democracies |
|---|---|---|---|
| SMD Plurality | 11.7[a] | 13.3[c] | 9.8[e] |
| PR | 3.7[b] | 4.8[d] | 2.9[f] |

*Key:* ID, Index of Disproportionality; PR, proportional representation; SMD, single-member district.

*Sources:* For Africa as a whole, author's calculations based partly on data presented in Shaheen Mozaffar, "The Political Origins and Consequences of Electoral Systems in Africa: A Preliminary Analysis" (paper presented at a conference on "Comparative Democratic Elections," Kennedy School of Government, Harvard University, May 12–14, 1995). For established democracies, calculations based on data presented in Arend Lijphart, *Electoral Systems and Party Systems* (New York: Oxford University Press, 1994), and updated by Reynolds.

*Note:* Method of calculation: least squares index developed by Michael Gallagher (1991).

[a]Thirteen elections: Botswana, 1965–94; Lesotho, 1993; Malawi, 1994; Zambia, 1991 and 1996; Zimbabwe, 1985 (common roll), 1990, 1995.

[b]Six elections: Angola, 1992; Mozambique, 1994; Namibia, 1989, 1994; South Africa, 1994; Zimbabwe 1980.

[c]Twenty elections: Botswana, 1965–94; Gambia, 1966–92; Kenya, 1992; Lesotho, 1993; Malawi, 1994; Zambia, 1991 and 1996; Zimbabwe, 1985–95.

[d]Thirteen elections: Angola, 1992; Benin, 1991; Burkina Faso, 1992; Burundi, 1993; Cape Verde, 1991; Madagascar, 1993; Mozambique, 1994; Namibia, 1989, 1994; Niger, 1993, 1995; South Africa, 1994; Zimbabwe, 1980.

[e]Calculated from data for 78 elections held under plurality in five countries: Canada, 1945–88; India, 1952–84; New Zealand, 1946–90; United Kingdom, 1945–92; United States, 1946–94.

[f]Calculated from data for 212 elections held under various PR formulas in 17 countries: Austria, 1945–90; Belgium, 1946–87; Costa Rica, 1953–90; Denmark, 1945–88; Finland, 1945–87; Germany, 1945–87; Iceland, 1946–87; Ireland, 1948–89; Israel, 1949–88; Italy, 1946–87; Luxembourg, 1945–89; Malta, 1947–87; Netherlands, 1946–89; Norway, 1945–89; Portugal, 1975–89; Sweden, 1948–88; Switzerland, 1947–87.

Second, if over the longer term economic and class mobility increases and ethnic and regional divisions fade, as most people hope, the resulting integration of neighborhoods and reduction in the political importance of primordial ties will likely bring about a decline in the geographic polarization of voting. This weakening of regional bloc voting will give rise to all the vagaries of plurality that more homogeneous societies such as Britain and the United States have been forced to endure. Such vagaries include the exclusion of substantially supported third parties from representation and the winning of parliamentary majorities by parties that have fewer votes than do their opponents. It is often claimed that while the more stable and established Western democracies can tolerate these representational anomalies, they could prove fatal in Africa, where democracy is—and will be for many years to come—fragile at best.

For example, if the Malawian Congress Party of former president Hastings Kamuzu Banda had won a parliamentary majority in 1994 with only 34 percent of the vote, against the 46 percent won by the United Democratic Front, one can only imagine the civil strife that would have erupted. Nor is this wild speculation without historical foundation. In the whites-only general election in South Africa in 1948, D. F. Malan's Nationalist–Afrikaner coalition came to power with 79 of the 150 seats in parliament despite polling only 42 percent of the vote. Jan Smuts's United–Labour coalition gained 52 percent of the popular vote but only 71 parliamentary seats.

Perhaps most important, the use of plurality in Southern Africa freezes the party system to such a degree that the alternation of parties in government and opposition is not perceived as a likely or natural occurrence. This is true even when levels of disproportionality are not high. As table 4-2 illustrates, elections held under SMD plurality in Southern Africa have provided a paucity of truly competitive seats—the lifeblood of the Westminster system of government.

All but two of the Southern African plurality elections described in table 4-2 reveal the classic elements of a de facto one-party state, in which governing parties are insulated from electoral challenges. In Lesotho, Malawi, Tanzania, Zambia, and Zimbabwe, the largest parties won their seats with huge segments of the vote, making them largely invulnerable for the most part. Marginal seats are those won with a margin of victory (whether a plurality or a majority) of less than 10 percent of the valid vote. These are considered "battleground seats"—which way they go determines which party forms a government. In the elections of the five established democracies, between one-fifth and one-third of the seats were considered marginal. In Southern Africa, however, competitive seats rarely amount to more than a tiny fraction of the legislative body. In Zimbabwe, no seat defended by a candidate of the incumbent

**Table 4-2.** Marginal Seats in Recent SMD Plurality Elections

| Election | No. of Marginals* | % of Total Seats | Largest Party | Average % Vote in Seats Won |
|---|---|---|---|---|
| ***Southern Africa*** | | | | |
| Zimbabwe 1995 | 0 | 0 | ZANU-PF | 82 |
| Lesotho 1993 | 0 | 0 | BCP | 75 |
| South Africa 1994 | 13 (5) | 3.2 | ANC | 80 |
| Zimbabwe 1990 | 4 (1) | 3.3 | ZANU-PF | 81 |
| Zimbabwe 1985 | 3 (1) | 3.7 | ZANU-PF | 91 |
| Zambia 1991 | 6 (4) | 4.0 | MMD | 81 |
| Malawi 1994 | 12 (5) | 6.8 | UDF | 72 |
| Namibia 1994 | 5 (2) | 6.9 | SWAPO | 85 |
| Zambia 1996 | 11 (7) | 7.3 | MMD | 66 |
| Tanzania 1995 | 23 (12) | 9.9 | CCM | 74 |
| Kenya 1992 | 30 (17) | 16.0 | KANU | 68 |
| Botswana 1994 | 8 (6) | 20.5 | BDP | 70 |
| ***Established Democ.*** | | | | |
| USA 1994 | 88 | 20.2 | Republican | 65 |
| Canada 1993 | 63 | 21.4 | Liberal | 56 |
| UK 1992 | 171 | 26.3 | Conservative | 52 |
| India 1980 | 157 | 29.7 | Congress | 52 |
| New Zealand 1993 | 30 | 30.3 | National | 44 |

* The number of marginal seats won by the largest party appears in parentheses. Marginal seats are defined as those seats won with a margin of victory of less than 10 percent of the total valid vote. Figures are for lower houses of parliament only.

*Key:* ANC, African National Congress; BCP, Basotho Congress Party; BDP, Botswana Democratic Party; CCM, Chama Cha Mapinduzi; KANU, Kenya African National Union; MMD, Movement for Multiparty Democracy; UDF, United Democratic Front; ZANU-PF, Zimbabwe African National Union–Patriotic Front.

party has ever changed hands. In effect, the use of plurality systems in heterogeneous societies *freezes* the number of seats won, creating an environment in which only a political earthquake can jar the patterns of party-vote concentration. Only in Kenya and Botswana have marginal seats reached the proportions necessary to indicate a degree of competitiveness within the system.

This finding rebuts the case for plurality in Africa, for such majoritarian prescriptions rely on at least the perception that power can change hands from election to election. If plurality leads to a de facto one-party state, there are no incentives for losing parties to remain loyal opposition parties. In the deeply divided societies of Africa, this poses the greatest possible threat to democracy in its initial stages. In contrast, PR systems may display sensitivity to evolving vote patterns by facilitating shifting government coalitions or forcing a single-party cabinet to include other parties when the ruling party's support falls below an absolute majority of the population.

## Remedying the Problems of PR

As Barkan points out, accountability and dialogue between representatives and constituents are crucial to any properly functioning democracy. And it is true that the type of national, large-district PR used in South Africa and Namibia has weakened the link between elites and nonelites, giving rise to fears of a "'suspended state' . . . disconnected from the population." Yet instituting an electoral system based on SMDs may not always be the best way to overcome such obstacles to the fulfillment of the vertical dimension of democracy. First, the overwhelmingly regional concentration of voting patterns throughout Africa gives rise to SMDs that are little more than pocket boroughs of one party or another. One intuitive hypothesis is that the less competitive the seat, the lower the quality of the candidates, and therefore the less responsive the elected MP will be to his or her constituents' needs. This "yellow dog" syndrome (so called because voters would sooner elect a yellow dog than someone from an opposing party) has been noted throughout the democracies that traditionally have used SMD plurality, especially the United States (where the term was coined) and the United Kingdom.

Second, adequate constituency representation is not simply a matter of advocating the interests of 50, 60, or even 80 percent of a given community; it is about allowing supporters of both majority and minority parties within a certain area to have their views articulated in parliament. In Africa, SMD plurality has accentuated regional fiefdoms of party dominance to the extent that 25 percent of the voters of Zambia's Eastern Province (who happened not to support the United National Independence Party in 1991), 15 percent of Malawi's Northern Region (who voted against the Alliance for Democracy), and virtually the entire opposition vote of Zimbabwe (which hovered around 19 percent in both 1990 and 1995) are prevented from having a direct say in legislative affairs. The constitutional engineer who seeks to craft a dynamic and inclusive representative democracy must look somewhere in between the extremes of the remote and unaccountable representation that characterizes national-list PR and the exclusionary and all too often complacent representation provided by MPs elected from "safe" SMDs.

The debate that took place within South Africa's Constitutional Assembly highlights both the dissatisfaction with large-district list PR and the ways in which PR systems can be adapted to provide more accountable and responsive representation. In South Africa, two options are now on the table. The first is to introduce SMDs for electing a proportion of the National Assembly (perhaps half), with the rest of the MPs being elected from regionally based lists. This would resemble the German system in that, overall, the National Assembly would reflect near proportionality between votes cast and seats won, but a single person would represent each district.

Although this "mixed-member" system might seem attractive, it has two key flaws. First, because of plurality's tendency to exaggerate regional fiefdoms, it is quite probable that certain parties would dominate all of the SMD seats, leaving minority-party MPs to be elected only from the "top-up" pool of members from regional lists. For example, throughout South Africa's Orange Free State, urban and rural constituencies would be represented solely by ANC members, while minority representatives would be elected from the more detached party lists. This leads to the second problem of the "mixed-member" system: the creation of two classes of MPs, the first group elected from districts tied to local parties and local voters and responsive to constituents' concerns, and the second group elected from the lists and therefore accountable chiefly to party bosses in national headquarters.

The second option is to reduce the size of the multimember districts of list PR and provide voters with more sophisticated choices on the ballot. In *Voting for a New South Africa* (Reynolds 1993: 66–103), I advocated a formula, akin to the Finnish system, by which 300 members of the South African National Assembly would be elected from MMDs ranging from five to twelve members in size, and voters could choose among candidates as well as parties. Parties would win seats in proportion to the number of votes they received, but those seats would be filled by the parties' most popular individual candidates. To ensure overall proportionality, 100 seats would be reserved to "top up" each party's share of the parliamentary seats; in order to remedy the problem of detachment, however, these additional members would be drawn from each party's most successful *losing* candidates.

This system is by no means perfect. Yet it retains overall proportionality in parliament and simplicity for the voter, while at the same time enhancing geographic accountability and diversity of representation within regions. An added benefit is that minority votes are not "wasted," as they are in SMD plurality; this might encourage minority parties in regions where one ethnic or linguistic group predominates. Minority representation and party organization within regions are particularly important when provincial powers are strengthened through federalism, as regional minorities are then less able to rely on the intervention of the national state to protect their interests.

## Conclusion

Joel Barkan and I agree on a number of important issues. We agree that choosing an electoral system involves a number of trade-offs among consequences that we attempt to predict by assessing evidence from previous elections. We concur that we should not seek a "perfect" electoral system, nor should we propagate one method as the single best system for any context. Rather, electoral rules must be tailored to the specific needs and desires of each individual society. Furthermore, we agree that the inclusion of both minority and majority interests, and therefore some degree of electoral proportionality, is a normative good in fledgling democracies that are divided along ethnic or regional lines.

I would argue, however, that the results of SMD-plurality elections throughout Africa and the rest of the world indicate that this system cannot be relied on to produce a distribution of parliamentary seats that closely mirrors the distribution of the popular vote, and thus will not necessarily facilitate a diverse and inclusive legislative body. Furthermore, plurality's potential to produce extremely disproportional results and legislative anomalies makes it especially unsuitable for the fragile new democracies of Africa. Barkan argues that electoral rules could be written so as to mandate culturally homogeneous districts (like the U.S. Justice Department's guidelines for racially representative districts), but my guess is that these legal gerrymanders would spark the same tension and controversy that have arisen in the United States.

Certainly, the list-PR systems currently in effect in Africa exhibit deficits of legitimacy and accountability. But there is no need to throw the baby out with the bathwater. With a little imagination and innovation, PR systems in Africa can be made to provide a solid link between representatives and constituents, thus strengthening the prospects for democratic consolidation. If South Africa, in devising its new constitution, finds a way to elect not only a proportional National Assembly but an accountable and responsive parliament representing all the people, it may again serve as a beacon for the rest of Africa.

# ELECTORAL SYSTEMS AND CONFLICT MANAGEMENT IN AFRICA
## A Twenty-Eight-State Comparison

Shaheen Mozaffar

This chapter analyzes the role of electoral systems in conflict management in Africa's emerging democracies. Two related questions frame the analysis: (1) Where do electoral systems come from? (2) What political consequences do they have?

The first question suggests the importance of a political logic behind the origin of electoral systems. Electoral systems are not engineered from preconceived blueprints, but are "born kicking and screaming into the world out of a messy, incremental compromise between contending factions battling for political survival, determined by power politics" (Norris 1995: 4). Electoral systems, in other words, reflect negotiated settlements of political conflicts over the institutional design of new democracies.

The second question directs attention to the political logic of electoral systems, that is, to their political consequences. Electoral systems, once in place, organize elections, influence the electoral goals, strategies, and behavior of political actors, and produce winners and losers. Electoral systems, in other words, structure political conflicts over distributional outcomes in democratic polities. Thus, they should demand attention from analysts and policymakers as they seek an instrument to manage such conflicts.

The chapter is divided into four sections. The first addresses the significance of elections as a mode of conflict management in democratic transitions. It also examines and rejects misplaced skepticism about the significance of elections in Africa's emerging democracies. The second section briefly traces the variations in the designs of new electoral systems in Africa to three analytically distinct patterns of choice, each featuring a distinct combination of political strategy and context that informed the institutional preferences of key political actors and constrained their bargaining strategies. The third section examines data on twenty-eight African electoral systems to assess their role in conflict management, especially through their impact on vote-seat disproportionality and the emerging party systems in Africa's new democracies.

This essay also directly addresses the debate in the previous two chapters between Andrew Reynolds and Joel Barkan over the appropriate designs of electoral systems in contemporary Africa. It suggests that this debate raises important and relevant questions, but closer empirical analysis of the workings of Africa's new electoral systems indicates a more complex reality than allowed by either position in the debate; specifically, the analysis cautions against unqualified acceptance of these positions. Both the Barkan-Reynolds debate and the analysis presented in this chapter raise some larger analytical issues, which are briefly addressed in the final section.

## Democratization and the Significance of Elections

Many analysts of Africa's rapid democratization, such as Claude Ake, are skeptical of the significance of elections as a means of conflict management (Ake 1991). Ake's skepticism, however, derives from an idealized vision of democratization as an emancipatory project—freeing the African peasant from the corrupt, self-practices of colonial and post-colonial elites—that is conceptually flawed and historically misconstrued. This vision puts the ideological cart before the historical horse, assuming a *prior commitment* by political elites to democratic values as the impulse behind the demand for democratization.

Lacking such commitment, political elites leading the current democratic reconstruction in Africa tend to regard democracy as a strategy for state power. They use elections to secure it by manipulating ignorant masses struggling to cope with economic deprivation. Based on a simplistic, or at least a contested, notion of democracy as popular power that treats the democratic commitment of the masses as unproblematic, this vision ignores the prior, very practical problem of devising rules embodying the mutual guarantees (Dahl 1989) that people make to each other when constituting (or reconstituting) a political community to constrain the potential excesses that are always inherent in the exercise of power.

Ake's emancipatory vision ignores the importance of rules composing institutions as cultural endowments that structure the exercise of power in public life. Hence, it confuses democratization with democracy. Democratization produces democracy. To produce democracy is to craft institutions. To craft institutions is to design rules that, in the first instance, authorize the restrained exercise of power in public life by *both* the governors and the governed. And to the extent these rules also encourage accommodation, compromise, and tolerance of diverse opinions, protracted functioning democracies *produce* rather than reflect a "civic" political culture (Karl and Schmitter 1991) in which emancipatory projects might evolve.

Ake's misplaced vision also leads to misdirected criticism of the significance of elections in African democratization.[1] Elections serve as cost-effective means to organize such contestation and extend the shadow of the future (Rawls 1971).[2] Elections are significant for two related reasons, both having to do with the comparative advantage of elections as a mode of collective decision making and conflict management vis-à-vis the structures of defunct autocracies. First, in contrast to the restricted opportunities of authoritarian regimes, elections provide generalized institutional opportunities of collective political choice. Second, precisely because they define the strategic context of political competition without determining its outcome, elections can productively engage individuals not as disembodied citizens, but as members of affinity groups.[3]

The process of negotiating ex ante agreements on new electoral rules, however, is fraught with conflict. This conflict, precisely because the outcomes of new rules are uncertain, involves the struggle of contending actors to design rules that they expect will secure their interests in the new democratic polity. Hence, the politics animating the choice of electoral systems, and of the overall institutional design of new democracies generally, becomes a process of conflict management. But attention to this dynamic of strategic choice alone offers no indication of the precise configuration of rules contending actors will negotiate to compose the new electoral systems. Institutional choice is tempered by the structural-historical context that defines the conflicting interests and power relations of contending actors, informs their institutional preferences, and constrains their strategies in bargaining over new electoral systems. How variations in this combination of strategy and context have produced variations in the institutional design of new electoral systems in Africa is examined in the next section.

## The Choice of Electoral Systems as Conflict Management

Three factors affect conflicts over the choice of electoral systems: electoral rules that convert votes into seats; the power relations and electoral expectations of political actors; and the structural-historical context that shapes these relations and expectations, informs the institutional preferences of political actors, and constrains their bargaining strategies over alternative electoral systems designs.

Conflicts over the choice of electoral systems are conflicts over political representation—specifically over maximum seat shares in legislative assemblies. Parties choose rules that they think will lead to winning elections, or at least maximizing their performance. The rules composing electoral systems affect the distribution of seat shares and are therefore the object of strategic bargaining. The comparative advantage of different electoral formulas in maximizing seat shares can be determined with reasonable accuracy from their mathematical properties,[4] increasing the cost of bargaining over new electoral rules.[5] Bargaining over rules of the electoral game is a key lever of conflict management.

The uncertainty that typically attends democratization as fundamental institutional transformation increases the salience of political actors' power relations and electoral expectations in shaping their institutional preferences rules and constraining their bargaining strategies (O'Donnell and Schmitter 1986; Przeworski 1991). However, as studies of the choice of electoral systems in both democracy's first wave in Western Europe (Carstairs 1980; Lipset and Rokkan 1967; Rokkan 1970) and its recent third wave in Asia, Latin America, and Southern and Eastern Europe (Brady and Mo 1992; Colomer 1995; Elster 1993; Lijphart 1992; Mainwaring 1991) have shown, political actors' power relations and electoral expectations are shaped by the institutional legacies of previous regimes. These legacies define the structural-historical context in which the configuration of social cleavages and attendant power relations of political actors combine to constrain their choice of alternative designs of new democratic institutions, producing distinct modes of democratization and different types of democracies (Karl 1990; Karl and Schmitter 1991).

In contemporary Africa, this combined influence of strategy and context is reflected in three broad patterns of democratization with corresponding variations in the choice of new electoral systems. Analytically, these three patterns can be classified as (a) the anglophone pattern, (b) the francophone pattern, and (c) the Southern Africa pattern.[6] Each pattern corresponds to distinct institutional arrangements of erstwhile authoritarian regimes and to their organization of political representation and constituency linkages—in particular, to the different ways in which authoritarian institutions structured and embedded the characteristic ethnoregional cleavages and socioeconomic divisions of African societies. These differences produced distinct patterns of state-society relations, with corresponding power asymmetries between and among state and societal actors, engendering different modes of democratization (Bratton and van de Walle 1994) and influencing the subsequent choice of different electoral systems.

### Anglophone Pattern

African authoritarian regimes were generally intolerant of autonomous associational life. Within this general pattern, however, the greater permissiveness of Anglophone authoritarian regimes enabled the organization of such entities as a farmers' association, an employers' association, ethnic welfare societies, and regional-, crop-, and industry-specific groupings separate from the ruling parties (Widner 1994: 54–56). In single-party regimes—notably, Kenya, Malawi, Tanzania, and Zambia—electoral opportunities were organized through multi-candidate electoral competition based on plurality formula in small geographically delimited single member districts (SMDs). Electoral opportunities were similarly organized in short-lived (Ghana, Nigeria, Sierra Leone) as well as in long-standing (Botswana, Gambia, Mauritius) democracies.[7]

These opportunities generally encouraged the development of strong constituency linkages based on pork-barrel servicing. They also enabled the development of extensive grassroots networks (soccer clubs in Ghana, for example) that helped to lower the cost of potential opposition candidates mounting a serious challenge to authoritarian incumbents, increasing the incumbents' risk of losing office and reducing their incentives to introduce multiparty democracies (Widner 1994: 55–56). But the very territorial fragmentation of local constituencies also increased the cost of sustaining a united national campaign for potential opponents. Authoritarian incumbents were thus generally able to manage the slow pace of democratic transitions in anglophone countries.[8]

In choosing new democratic institutions, both authoritarian incumbents and opposition groups, expecting to preserve their respective established local power bases while dividing their opponents, converged on plurality formula and SMDs as the preferred allocative formula for the new electoral systems. For authoritarian incumbents, small territorial districts would preserve their traditional strongholds, and plurality rule would give their parties' candidates an advantage over the typically numerous opposition candidates, while fragmenting opposition parties, preventing them from forming legislative majorities, and enhancing the ability of the now democratically elected authoritarian rulers in coopting individual opposition members to form a government should the ruling parties fail to win legislative majorities.

Similarly, for opposition groups, plurality formula and SMDs not only would preserve their traditional local power bases, but also would enable them to form a government by coopting individual ruling and other opposition party members should the fragmented opposition parties fail to win legislative majorities. This was a major reason why, in Ghana's democratic transition, opposition as well as government-appointed members of the Consultative Assembly charged with devising a new constitution roundly rejected the German-style additional member system that was proposed by the Committee of Experts appointed by the incumbent Rawlings regime. Finally, for both authoritarian incumbents and their democratic opponents, plurality SMDs also provided the institutional means to accommodate localized subregional and subethnic cleavages and personalist factions that traditionally characterize African political parties. Such accommodation becomes especially important in maintaining party unity when there is a small number of large parties and each party's electoral support is ethnoregionally concentrated, as, for example, in Malawi.

### Francophone Pattern

Authoritarian regimes in francophone countries typically favored corporatist modes of interest mediation. Specified social and economic interests (producers' associations, labor, students, women, teachers, civil servants) were formally organized into state-sponsored peak associations, approximating representational monopolies usually tied to ruling parties (Widner 1994: 54; also see Robinson 1991). Electoral opportunities in these regimes were organized through single national party lists tightly controlled by central party elites. Elections were held mostly in large multimember districts by plurality formula. These opportunities created disincentives for ambitious politicians to establish strong constituency linkages, deflecting their efforts to seeking favor with central party elites who controlled valuable institutional (media, candidate selection, patronage) and financial resources. In the recent wave of democratization, corporate groups allied to single-party regimes were able to use the very corporatist structures through which they were organized to reduce collection actions costs and spearhead the popular movements that quickly toppled reluctant autocrats (Bratton and van de Walle 1992; Widner 1994).

In most francophone countries, the politics of institutional choice was played out in the broad-based National Conferences that assumed sovereign power following the collapse of authoritarian regimes (Robinson 1994). In most cases, the presence of equally balanced groups in the National Conference led to a strategic convergence on proportional representation (PR) as the preferred allocative formula for the new electoral systems. The inclusion of all major social forces in choosing new democratic institutions meant that no group was singularly dominant to impose its preferred institutional outcome, and hence no single group could be confident of securing decisive legislative majorities in competitive elections. For the groups previously allied to defunct authoritarian regimes, moreover, the loss of incumbency removed a key institutional advantage and underlined their uncertain electoral prospects in unfamiliar electoral competition. Hence, each group had the incentive to support PR formulas to ensure some legislative representation for all.

Variations in power relations and electoral expectations associated with variations in the organized representation of social groups also account for the choice of two-round majoritarian formulas, typified by Mali, as well as for the choice of two-tiered electoral system with combined plurality-PR formulas, typified by Senegal. In Mali, of the 47 political parties that emerged during that country's rather chaotic democratic transition, only three had anything approximating a national base. A second tier of parties were largely regionally based, but had the potential for becoming national parties. Below these groups were numerous smaller parties with predominantly regional and local bases, with no prospect of entering the national government without coalescing with the larger parties. The resulting debate over the design of a new electoral system produced a two-round majority formula for National Assembly elections at the insistence of the larger parties, interested in preserving their electoral advantage. These parties, however, agreed to a PR formula with a very low threshold for municipal elections to accommodate the demands of the smaller parties for representation (Vengroff 1993, 1994).

The choice of Senegal's complex two-tiered electoral system not only attests to the effects of correlated variations in the strategic calculations of political actors and in the organized representation of social groups on institutional outcomes, but also underscores the strategic constraints authoritarian rulers face both from opposition groups in society and from within the single parties they lead.[9] The ruling Socialist Party (PS) in Senegal, like its counterpart in other former single-party regimes in Africa, was not a unified organization, but a coalition of divergent interests likely to suffer political losses from any change in electoral rules favoring opposition groups. The choice of Senegal's complex two-tiered electoral system was structured by these constraints, reflected specifically in the triangular power relations among the competing patronage networks within the PS, between the PS and the Senegalese Democratic Party (PDS), the dominant opposition party, and between the PDS and the numerous smaller opposition parties.

Abdou Diouf's preemptive political reforms in 1983 were aimed as much at accommodating opposition demands for political liberalization as at weakening Leopold Senghor's increasingly unpopular holdout "barons" dominating the PS hierarchy. The unlimited pluralism introduced by the reforms subjected them to the uncertainties of unfamiliar electoral competition, enabling Diouf to create his own patronage networks.[10] These rule changes led to a steady gain in the seat shares of opposition parties from 7 percent in 1983 to 14 percent in 1988 to 30 percent in 1993. The advantage accruing to opposition groups by the PR allocations of seats, especially by the increase in these seats from 60 to 70 in 1993, was particularly significant. While the PS won 47 percent of its seats under PR rules in 1993, the opposition parties won 83 percent of their seats under the same rules. The PDS was the single biggest winner, securing 77 percent of its seats by PR allocation.

### Southern African Pattern

The combination of strategy and context influencing the choice of new electoral systems in Angola, Mozambique, Namibia, and South Africa distinguishes the Southern Africa pattern. Civil wars in Angola, Namibia, and Mozambique, and widespread civil unrest and political violence in South Africa, defined the context for the protracted strategic negotiations among contending groups of actors that animated the choice of new electoral systems. In all four countries, these negotiations were aimed at accommodating the conflicting interests of contending actors divided by ethnoregional (Angola and Mozambique) and racial (Namibia and South Africa) cleavages. These cleavages were themselves the institutional legacies of the authoritarian regimes established at the conclusion of successful national liberation wars in Angola and Mozambique and of the apartheid regimes in Namibia and South Africa.

Protracted negotiations in all four countries produced PR systems, but of different types that correlated with the conflicting groups' power relations and electoral expectations. In Angola and Mozambique, where a polarized ethnoregional cleavage provided safe electoral constituencies for conflicting groups, strategic negotiations produced a d'Hondt system, the least proportional of PR formulas, that privileged the two major parties in each country (MPLA [Popular Movement for the Liberation of Angola] and UNITA in Angola, Frelimo and Renamo in Mozambique), effectively shutting out the smaller parties. In Namibia and South Africa, where white minorities with economic and political power confronted disenfranchised black majorities, strategic negotiations aimed at devising inclusive institutional settlements that encouraged power sharing produced two of the more proportional PR formulas, LR-Hare in Namibia and LR-Droop in South Africa (LR being largest remainder).

The choices of the electoral system governing Zimbabwe's 1980 independence elections and of the proposed electoral system for Sierra Leone's scheduled elections in January 1996 reflect variants of the Southern Africa pattern. In both countries, negotiated democratic settlements in the context of civil war led to the choice of PR formula to accommodate the representation of the major contending actors. In Zimbabwe, the rules for the 1980 elections were contained in the Transitional Provisions of the Lancaster House Agreement and provided, among other features, a one-hundred-seat House of Assembly, of which eighty seats were elected by LR-Hare formula by black and white voters on a common roll in eight multimember constituencies (corresponding to the country's eight administrative districts) with magnitudes ranging from six to sixteen, and twenty seats were elected in single member districts by majority formula with single transferable vote (STV) by white voters registered on a white roll. These provisions were negotiated as interim measures, pending the drawing of new single member constituencies, which was accomplished for the 1985 elections (Gregory 1981; Moyo 1992).

Finally, in Sierra Leone, a PR formula is widely agreed to be an effective institutional device for including the conflicting parties in what is likely to be a government of national unity.[11] While the prospect of holding the scheduled elections in January 1996 remains uncertain at present, given the continued civil war in parts of the country, the choice of the LR-Hare formula for allocating seats reflects a pragmatic response to the need to enhance the perceived legitimacy of elections as a mode of peaceful conflict management, to reduce political tensions, and to establish minimum conditions for political stability. More generally, the preference for a PR formula in a country which has traditionally relied on the first-past-the-post system indicates that the choice of electoral rules is neither historically determined nor culturally prescribed, but represents a rational response tempered by political calculations in changing contexts.

## The Impact of Electoral Systems on Conflict Management

Electoral systems manage social conflicts by defining the strategic context for their political organization, expression, and representation. Variations in this definition, and hence variations in how electoral systems manage social conflicts and shape political outcomes, depend on variations in two key institutional dimensions of electoral systems that convert votes into seats: electoral formula and district magnitude (Lijphart 1994; Taagepera and Shugart 1989).[12]

All electoral formulas introduce disparity between votes and seats, and all discriminate against smaller parties, but some do so more than others. The key is the number of votes required to win one seat: the greater the number of votes required per seat, the greater the discriminatory effects and hence the greater the barrier to securing representation for divergent interests. In general, majoritarian-plurality formulas require more votes to win one seat than PR formulas. Within PR formulas, those based on largest remainders (LR-Hare and LR-Droop) tend to require a smaller percentage of votes to win one seat than those based on highest averages (d'Hondt and Sainte-Lague).[13] District magnitude refers to the number of seats available for allocation. The larger the district magnitude, the greater the opportunity for divergent interests to secure representation.

Political parties are central to the political organization of conflicts associated with the pattern of social cleavages and issue dimensions in the wider society (Duverger 1963; Lijphart 1984: 127–149). But the ability of political parties to organize conflicting interests in the electoral process and secure their legislative representation depends on the simplifying effects of electoral formulas and district magnitude. These effects can be measured by the degree of disproportionality between votes and seats and by the resulting degree of fragmentation in the party system.

Tables 5-1 through 5-4 present data for twenty-eight African electoral systems on the effects of electoral formula and effective threshold (a surrogate variable for district magnitude) on vote-seat disproportionality, on the effective numbers of electoral parties (parties competing in elections), and on the effective numbers of assembly parties (parties winning legislative seats).[14] In table 5-1, the data displayed in the right-hand column indicate that as effective thresholds increase (or district magnitude decreases), the vote-seat disproportionality increases as well, although the trend is not monotonic. Data displayed in the bottom row indicate the monotonic effect of electoral formulas on vote-seat disproportionality, aside from the LR-Droop formula used in South Africa (the only one in Africa). *While the PR formulas are generally more proportional than the majoritarian-plurality formulas, African electoral systems using the LR-Hare quota, the most proportional of all PR formulas, tend to be almost twice as proportional as the majoritarian-plurality formulas.* For all PR systems, the average LSq (least-squares) index is 7.42, compared with the average of 11.87 for SMD plurality systems.[15]

Because vote-seat disproportionality affects the structure of the party system, and given the importance of parties in the political organization and in representation of social conflicts, a direct

**Table 5-1.** Average Percentages of Vote-Seat Disproportionality Classified by Electoral Formula and Effective Threshold for Twenty-eight African Electoral Systems

| Effective Threshold (%) | LR-Hare | LR-Droop | d'Hondt | Plurality | Majority/ Plurality | ALL |
|---|---|---|---|---|---|---|
| 0.18–1.66 | 11.40 (2) | 0.30 (1) | 3.87 (1) | – | – | 6.74 (4) |
| 5.00–9.00 | 13.30 (2) | – | 7.91 (2) | – | – | 10.60 (4) |
| 10.00–19.00 | 5.32 (2) | – | 11.98 (2) | – | – | 8.65 (4) |
| 20.83–29.17 | 0.55 (2) | – | – | 17.39 (1) | 23.28 (1) | 10.30 (4) |
| 35 | – | – | – | 11.36 (11) | 3.61 (1) | 10.72 (12) |
| ALL | 7.64 (8) | 0.30 (1) | 8.73 (5) | 11.87 (12) | 13.45 (2) | 9.80 (28) |

*Note:* The number of cases on which the average percentages are based is in parentheses.

comparison of the number of parties competing in elections with the number of parties winning seats offers additional insight into the political consequences of electoral systems for conflict management. The data displayed in tables 5-2, 5-3, and 5-4 present this comparison. *They lend broad support to the thesis that PR formulas, combined with lower effective thresholds, tend to encourage more parties to compete in elections and to enable them to win seats.* Almost the same number of parties win seats as compete in elections in systems using the LR-Hare formula, with the reduction between electoral parties and assembly parties increasing with systems using increasingly discriminatory formulas (again, ignoring the single case of the highly proportional LR-Droop formula in South Africa's).[16]

These data, in general, confirm the expected differences in the political outcomes of electoral systems. They also provide broad support to Reynolds's position in his debate with Barkan over the appropriate designs of electoral systems in Africa's emerging

**Table 5-2.** Average Effective Numbers of Electoral Parties Classified by Electoral Formula and Effective Threshold for Twenty-eight African Electoral Systems

| Effective Threshold (%) | LR-Hare | LR-Droop | d'Hondt | Plurality | Majority/Plurality | ALL |
|---|---|---|---|---|---|---|
| 0.18–1.66 | 2.00 (2) | 2.2 (1) | 2.5 (1) | – | – | 2.2 (4) |
| 5.00–9.00 | 5.7 (2) | – | 2.3 (2) | – | – | 4.0 (4) |
| 10.00–19.00 | 3.5 (2) | – | 2.7 (2) | – | – | 3.1 (4) |
| 20.83–29.17 | 4.3 (2) | – | – | 2.2 (1) | 4.6 (1) | 3.9 (3) |
| 35 | – | – | – | 2.3 (11) | 2.1 (1) | 2.3 (12) |
| ALL | 3.9 (8) | 2.2 (1) | 2.5 (5) | 2.3 (12) | 3.4 (2) | 2.9 (28) |

*Note:* The number of cases on which the average effective numbers of electoral parties are based is in parentheses.

**Table 5-3.** Average Effective Numbers of Assembly Parties Classified by Formula and Effective Threshold for Twenty-eight African Electoral Systems

| Effective Threshold (%) | LR-Hare | LR-Droop | d'Hondt | Plurality | Majority/Plurality | ALL |
|---|---|---|---|---|---|---|
| 0.18–1.66 | 1.6 (2) | 2.2 (1) | 2.2 (1) | – | – | 1.9 (4) |
| 5.00–9.00 | 4.9 (2) | – | 1.8 (2) | – | – | 3.3 (4) |
| 10.00–19.00 | 3.0 (2) | – | 1.8 (2) | – | – | 2.4 (4) |
| 20.83–29.17 | 4.3 (2) | – | – | 1.7 (1) | 2.2 (1) | 3.1 (4) |
| 35 | – | – | – | 1.8 (11) | 2.1 (1) | 1.8 (12) |
| ALL | 3.4 (8) | 2.2 (1) | 1.9 (5) | 1.8 (12) | 2.2 (2) | 2.3 (28) |

*Note:* The number of cases on which the average effective numbers of assembly parties are based is in parentheses.

**Table 5-4.** Contextual Effects on the Political Outcomes of Electoral Systems

| Electoral Formula | Social Structure | |
| --- | --- | --- |
| | Polarized | Fragmented |
| LR-Hare | Mirror Effect | Reductive Effect |
| | *Ex: Namibia* <br> *LSq = 1.1* <br> $N_v = 2.1$ <br> $N_s = 2.1$ | *Ex: Madagascar* <br> *LSq = 0.0* <br> $N_v = 6.5$ <br> $N_s = 6.5$ |
| d'Hondt | Mirror Effect | Reductive Effect |
| | *Ex: Burundi* <br> *LSq = 5.96* <br> $N_v = 1.7$ <br> $N_s = 1.5$ | *Ex: Burkina Faso* <br> *LSq = 18.95* <br> $N_v = 3.6$ <br> $N_s = 1.8$ |
| Plurality | Mirror Effect | Reductive Effect |
| | *Ex: Malawi* <br> *LSq = 2.00* <br> $N_v = 2.7$ <br> $N_s = 2.7$ | *Ex: Kenya* <br> *LSq = 18.38* <br> $N_v = 4.1$ <br> $N_s = 2.8$ |

democracies. But they do not offer a basis to close this debate. Instead, they warrant caution about, and suggest modifications to, the explanations and conclusions Barkan and Reynolds advance with respect to the workings and the political outcomes of Africa's new electoral systems.

## Beyond the PR-Plurality Debate

If the debate over the appropriate electoral system design for Africa's emerging democracies is to move beyond mere heuristic academic exercise, then it must begin by reformulating the question from which electoral system *ought* to be chosen to which is *likely* to be chosen.[17] This reformulation recognizes that electoral systems, like all institutions, are chosen in the context of existing institutional arrangements, and they are embedded power asymmetries that shape the preferences of political actors about the new electoral rules and constrain their bargaining strategies over alternative rule configurations. In this respect, the Barkan-Reynolds debate reflects the heretofore dominant tendency in extant scholarship to emphasize the political *outcomes* of electoral systems designs as the prescriptive criteria for the choice of these designs (Lijphart and Grofman 1984; Sartori 1968, 1994). With the global advance of democracy, scholarly attention has now appropriately shifted to clarifying the political logic that motivates the choice of alternative electoral systems (Brady and Mo 1992; Colomer 1994, 1995; Lijphart 1992; Mainwaring 1991).[18]

This shift in analytical focus has two implications. First, it avoids (at least, it should) the methodologically suspect comparison of the effects of new electoral systems in Africa, and in other third wave democracies, with the effects of electoral systems in established democracies, a strategy that Barkan and Reynolds follow. A more useful comparative insight for clarifying the potential for the consolidation of new electoral systems and the emerging party systems, and hence for democratic consolidation, in contemporary Africa can be gleaned from the process of democratization and subsequent democratic consolidation in nineteenth century Western Europe.[19]

In Europe, democratization represented a means to accommodate conflicts engendered by the twin processes of nation-building and industrialization. The initial electoral systems were all based on the majority principle, which led to considerable fluctuations in the vote distributions of new political parties, but also to regular alternation of governments between them. PR systems were then introduced for two reasons. The first was similar to the reasons why PR is adopted in many ethnically divided societies in contemporary Africa and other third world regions, to accommodate the concerns of linguistic and ethnic minorities of being consigned to permanent minority positions in majoritarian systems (Denmark in 1855, Swiss canton in 1891, Belgium in 1899, Finland in 1906).

The second reason was a convergence of interests between the rising working class, which demanded universal suffrage and a lower threshold to secure legislative representation denied them under majoritarian formulas based on restricted franchise, and the old established parties, which wanted to protect their legislative representation in return for their support of working-class demands (Rokkan 1970: 157). Where PR was introduced, democratic stability was secured by the inclusion of otherwise threatened political parties, such as the Liberal Party in Belgium. Where it was not introduced, it led to the extinction of some parties, such as the Liberal Party in Britain (Duverger 1963).

This Western European experience suggests that some form of representation equity is a key to securing the legitimacy of new democracies. To the extent that African plurality systems engender equitable representation, either through coalitions (as in Malawi) or through regular party alternation in government (to date, Mauritius and São Tomé et Principe remain notable exceptions in this respect, and the latter has experienced only one such alternation), the potential for democratic consolidation is likely to be enhanced in these systems. PR systems clearly remain superior in securing equitable representation, but they pose dilemmas in forming effective governments (Madagascar), in sustaining precariously balanced coalition governments (Benin and Niger), or in establishing effective vertical links between voter and representative, as Barkan points out. These dilemmas are inherent in all democracies, and no electoral system can entirely resolve them (Huber and Powell 1994). But their peaceful management is a matter of institutional crafting to mold a process of strategic learning that takes time.

Hence, the second implication of the shift in analytical focus noted above is the need for more systematic attention to the temporal dimension of democratic consolidation. Here also, the Western European experience offers useful insight. The institutionalized electoral systems in established democracies embody widely accepted norms of electoral behavior (victory does not mean permanent monopoly of power, nor does defeat imply political obscurity, or worse) that serve to mitigate the effects of disproportional outcomes.[20] That such norms have not yet developed in contemporary Africa cannot be denied. But in established democracies, as well, these norms developed over time. They developed through the adjustment of political parties to the unintended consequences of electoral systems.

But, more importantly, they developed through a variety of formal and informal mechanisms (such as the committees and seniority systems in the United States Congress) devised by political leaders to manage the inherent tension between representation and governance. To the extent that elections remain a viable means of peaceful conflict management—that is, to the extent they provide effective avenues for representation of conflicting interests and for peaceful change in government—Duverger's psychological effects work to stabilize electoral outcomes over several electoral cycles. Most of Africa's new democracies have yet to go through these cycles. In the meantime, discontent with present electoral systems and their political outcomes is not likely to fade away.

But the response to this discontent also reveals political creativity and sensitivity. In South Africa, the African National Congress has established an informal constituency-servicing mechanism by assigning MPs and cabinet ministers to designated areas and providing them with the necessary funds to maintain a presence there (Barkan 1995: 111). And in Mali, both government and opposition MPs have informally divided up their multimember districts into personal constituency-servicing bailiwicks (Vengroff 1993). These strategies represent pragmatic adjustments to the tension between representation and governance inherent in all democracies.

# ■ PART III: Cases

The two essays that follow offer a case-study approach to the overall issues raised in this volume. In chapter 6, Emmanuel Gyimah-Boadi offers insights into a successful election—Ghana's second transitional election of December 1996—and illustrates how election-related conflicts were managed through formal and informal processes. In contrast to the other essays in this volume, Gyimah-Boadi's turns our attention to the importance of administrative procedures and processes for managing election-related conflict.

In chapter 7, Robert B. Mattes and Amanda Gouws provide an analysis of voter behavior in South Africa's 1994 election, which was open to all races for the first time, to illustrate that the assumptions often made by scholars and policymakers alike—in this case, that voting in a highly conflicted multiethnic society is tantamount to an "ethnic census"—are often misplaced. They relate public opinion data to the issue of appropriate electoral system choice. These essays provide both depth and texture to the analysis of elections and conflict management.

# 6

# MANAGING ELECTORAL CONFLICTS
## Lessons from Ghana

Emmanuel Gyimah-Boadi

It is true, as many of the essays in this volume take for granted, that elections are highly institutionalized procedures for the resolution of political conflict in a democracy. It is also true that the continent's authoritarian rulers and their supporters have had self-serving motives in exaggerating the conflict-generating or conflict-intensifying aspects of elections, and that the appearance of peace and stability under autocratic regimes was often superficial and transient. However, the relatively few episodes of multiparty elections in the multinational and inadequately integrated post-colonial African states have tended to generate intense conflicts. Moreover, transition elections (which is what African elections of the 1990s really are), though highly crucial to the installation and consolidation of democracy, are inherently prone to intense competition, disputation, and other developments that heighten conflict.

While transition elections have facilitated the ending of civil wars in Mali, Mozambique, Sierra Leone, and South Africa, they have intensified conflicts in Angola and Nigeria. As African countries have come to commit themselves to democracy in the 1990s, it would be highly imprudent to ignore the conflict-generating potential of multiparty elections. Indeed, the design of mechanisms for managing conflicts, including electoral ones in multinational and poorly integrated African countries, should be an intrinsic part of the project of democratizing the continent.

The relative success of Ghana's second transition election in December 1996[1] provides a good opportunity to gain lessons and insights into how electoral systems may be designed and administered to minimize conflicts in elections and disputes over their outcomes, and thereby to improve the prospects for democratic consolidation. Despite Ghana's history of electoral conflicts (especially in 1956 and 1978),[2] and despite widespread fears of pre- and post-election violence,[3] polling in Ghana on December 7, 1996, was very peaceful, and the results were broadly accepted by the public. This chapter analyzes the management of the Ghanaian presidential and parliamentary elections of December 1996 and reviews the formal and informal ways by which conflict was moderated and the prospects for that country's young democracy were thereby enhanced. The final section discusses unresolved issues and problems in Ghana's quest to institutionalize electoral fairness and to entrench conflict resolution in its electoral and democratic processes.

## Background to the December 1996 Elections in Ghana

The causes of political conflicts and violence in Ghanaian politics are certainly complex and multifaceted. But, at least in a superficial sense, the elections of November and December 1992 were a major source of intense conflict in Ghanaian politics in that period. Indeed, the elections and their immediate aftermath seemed to validate claims persistently advanced by authoritarian rulers, their allies, and enemies of liberal democratic government in Ghana that competitive elections provoked unnecessary tensions and conflicts, and that they posed a threat to the unity and economic development of the country. The elections were dogged by threats to peace, ranging from the macabre to the melodramatic. These included post-election violence such as the detonation of four bombs in different parts of Accra by a shadowy group called Alliance of Democratic Forces (ADF); the politically motivated burning to death of the chairman of the western region branch of the ruling National Democratic Congress (NDC); rioting in Kumasi by supporters of the main opposition party—the New Patriotic Party (NPP)—following the declaration of the NDC as the winner of the presidential polls; the subsequent imposition of a dusk-to-dawn curfew in the Ashanti region; and demonstrations in protest against the alleged rigging of the elections in the city center of Accra by seminude female supporters of the NPP.

But perhaps the greatest challenge to Ghana's transition to democracy was presented by the nonviolent protest of the main opposition parties—the New Patriotic Party, the National Independence Party (NIP), the People's National Convention (PNC), and the Heritage Party. A decision by these parties to boycott the parliamentary elections in December 1992 led to the establishment of a de facto one-party parliament.[4] This in turn created a legitimacy problem for many of the key institutions of democratic politics and the peaceful management of political conflicts in the fourth Republic. Political opposition took an extra-parliamentary form, and relations between the government and its opposition became deeply acrimonious. In addition, many of the very constitutional bodies established to foster peace, reconciliation, and political tolerance, such as the Media Commission, the National Commission on Civic Education, the Commission on Human Rights and Administrative Justice, the National Electoral Commission, and the Judiciary (especially the Supreme Court), came under severe attack by opposition elements resentful over the fact that the heads and other key officials of such institutions had been appointed without adequate consultation outside of the ruling regime.

When communal conflicts, notably in northeastern Ghana, degenerated into violence with significant loss of life in February 1994, and when riots rocked the major cities of Ghana in protest over the introduction of a value-added tax in May 1995, it appeared the worst prediction that political liberalization and multiparty competition would give rise to conflicts in Ghanaian society had come true. The sections below discuss the main problems in the administration of the 1992 elections and review the measures taken to resolve them and to pave the way for relatively peaceful elections and acceptable outcomes in 1996.

**Problems in the 1992 Elections**

Because the 1992 elections were intended as a transition to end a decade of military rule and usher the country into civilian, constitutional governance, the administration of these elections posed some peculiar problems.

- Acute time constraints hindered the Interim National Electoral Commission (INEC)'s efforts to prepare adequately for the elections, to manage election logistics, and to plan and work out details of electoral events.

  INEC conducted a referendum on a new draft constitution for Ghana's fourth Republic on April 28, 1992. In the referendum, the people were asked not only to approve or reject the new constitution, but also to agree on January 7, 1993 as the date for a return to constitutional rule. Subsequent to the referendum, on May 15, 1992, the ban on political party activity, in force since 1982, was lifted. This paved the way for the formation of political parties and their registration by INEC once they satisfied certain requirements laid down in law. The first political party received certification in mid-July, 1992. Meanwhile, the presidential election had been scheduled for November 3, and legislative elections for December 8, 1992. This meant that even the first party to receive certification had barely four months to prepare for the elections.

- The electoral mechanism had gone unused for a decade, except for staggered local-level elections in 1988–89, and the mechanism was therefore rusty.

  Key among the problems were the flawed nature of the existing voters' register (electoral roll), which had been compiled originally in 1987 and not updated since, the absence of reliable population figures and information on where people lived, and the absence of a firm demographic basis for determining the distribution of voters for purposes of siting polling stations. Consequently, some duly registered voters were disenfranchised because they could not find their polling stations on election day, creating suspicions that INEC and the incumbent regime had connived to disenfranchise opposition voters.

- Logistical problems arose on election day, caused by the short time available for the procurement of the election supplies and delays in resource mobilization, which affected distribution of election materials on schedule.

- Time and resource constraints adversely affected the capacity of the election authority to carry out effectively the important tasks of educating the electorate on voting procedures and the necessity to exercise their franchise; educating thousands of election personnel on the laws and regulations governing the elections; and training those personnel in the technical aspects of the administration of the elections. Noticeably, election officials made mistakes or failed to follow proper procedures on election day, casting doubt on the credibility of the election process.

- Widespread mistrust and suspicion among oppositional groups in the country about the independence and neutrality of INEC in discharging its responsibilities for the electoral aspects of the transitional program had to be addressed.

  The suspicion arose at least in part from the fact that the incumbent government—the Provisional National Defense Council (PNDC)—unilaterally appointed the members of INEC without consulting opposition elements. These suspicions were heightened when Flight Lieutenant Jerry Rawlings, the head of that government, decided to contest the presidential election as a civilian. As a candidate, he enjoyed clear advantages of incumbency and visibility over his rivals, thus raising doubts about a level playing field.

One upshot of these problems was that the election authority found itself having to administer a crowded program of electoral events, with a high probability of shortcomings and imperfections on election day. Another was that the newly formed political parties had little time to get off the ground and the candidates to mount credible campaigns. It is not surprising, then, that the result of the presidential elections, which brought Rawlings to power as the first president of the fourth Republic, was vehemently rejected by his opponents, even though a number of international observer groups gave an overall positive rating to the actual conduct of the election. Citing the defective register, the losing candidates and parties made a host of unsubstantiated allegations covering every conceivable irregularity and fraud in the election code.[5] They included intimidation and interference by security personnel and "revolutionary" organs; multiple voting, impersonation, and ineligible voters; pre-stuffed ballot boxes and ballot dumping; bribery and other corrupt practices; and collaboration and collusion with the electoral authority. Instead of going to court for the resolution of their grievances as permitted by the election law, the losing parties decided to boycott the legislative elections eventually held on December 28, 1992, resulting in a one-party first parliament of the fourth Republic.

## Preparing for the 1996 Elections

With the inauguration of the fourth Republic, the life of INEC officially came to an end. A new Electoral Commission (EC) was inaugurated in August 1993 (see the section on resolving ethnic conflict below).[6] The new commission decided to reform the electoral system against the backdrop of events surrounding the 1992 elections. It recognized that the row over the results, and the compendium of allegations of fraud (many of them unsubstantiated), had left in their trail lingering suspicion and mistrust of the election authority as an independent and impartial arbiter of democratic elections, and a battered faith in the ballot box. Above all, it saw a clear need for electoral reforms with a view to achieving greater transparency in all aspects of the election process. In addition, it sought to create popular faith in the ballot box as the arbiter of a democratic electoral contest, to eliminate or at least minimize dispute over election outcomes, and, as a by-product, to build confidence in the commission. In practice, it meant the new commission had to undertake the following tasks:

- Address the legitimate concerns of the political parties about the shortcomings of the 1992 elections, especially the main demands made by the losing parties in the aftermath of the elections as a condition for their participation in any future elections. These demands included the compilation of a new voter register, copies of which must be given to the losing parties well ahead of elections, the issuing of identity cards to all registered voters, the holding of presidential and parliamentary elections on the same day, and the use of transparent ballot boxes.

- Develop a more comprehensive program of voter education.
- Provide better training for election officials.
- Plan electoral events in more detail well ahead of election time and in a more organized fashion.

### Registration of Voters

An entirely new voter register was compiled to replace the flawed one used for the 1992 elections. This time, the political parties were actively involved in the planning and implementation of the registration exercise, in a collective effort to create a comprehensive, accurate, and reliable register. After thorough discussions with the political parties, a consensus was reached on the design of the registration form, the structure and contents of the register, the methods for compiling it, and related matters. The parties were allowed four agents or monitors (two for the parties in government and two for the nongovernment parties) at each registration center during the entire fifteen-day registration period. The agents were trained by the EC alongside its own registration officials to ensure that both official and agent understood the process.

Registration took place at 20,000 centers nationwide. At each center, daily records of the number of persons registered were kept, signed by the registration officer and counter-signed by the party agents. The agents, like every citizen, could challenge a person applying for registration on the ground that he or she was not qualified according to the requirements laid down. Such challenges were decided by district-based registration review committees on which political party representatives sat, and a person aggrieved by a committee's decision had a right of appeal to the high court. Altogether, 9.2 million people registered as voters, of whom 49.7 percent were women. Each elector was given an ID card with a unique number. To make it easy for people to identify their polling stations, the place where a person registered was designated as his or her polling station on election day, and the station number was printed on the ID Card.

After the field collection of the registration data, scanning technology was used in compiling the register as a means of cutting down on time and errors in computer data entry. A two-week period of exhibition (public scrutiny) of the register at the 20,000 registration centers/polling stations followed the compilation of the provisional register. During the exhibition, objections could still be made to unqualified names in the register. Such objections were resolved by district judicial officers, although an aggrieved person had a right of appeal to the high court. At the exhibition, 6.5 million, or 73 percent, of all the registered voters checked their particulars. Copies of the final register of voters were given to the political parties in both paper and computer-readable (CD Rom) form.

### Training of Election Officials and Party Agents

To ensure that election officials clearly understood the rules and regulations governing the elections and followed proper procedures, the EC wrote down detailed, step-by-step procedures to be followed by each category of election official. This step was buttressed by practical, hands-on training designed to give the various categories of officials experience in what they were required to do in connection with the elections. After their training, the officials were sworn by a judicial officer to faithfully execute the election law.

Additionally, since by law every candidate contesting an election was entitled to appoint an agent to represent him or her at each polling station, the training program was expanded to include candidates' or party agents. Like the election officials, the party agents were required to take an oath to uphold the election laws and regulations and to sign the polling station results form (or otherwise give reasons in writing for failing to do so) and to receive a certified copy for their candidates. In this way any challenges to the results could be easily verified and resolved. Knowledgeable party agents who witnessed the relevant activities before, during, and after polling were particularly well-placed to testify to the credibility of the election.

## Public Education

To reduce widespread misunderstandings and suspicions about the election process, which led people to believe allegations of impropriety and wrongdoing in the administration of elections, the commission embarked on a public education program that went beyond familiarizing the voting public with the mechanics of voting to providing basic information about the election process. The idea was that an electorate sufficiently knowledgeable about the do's and don't's of elections would be better able to evaluate allegations of impropriety and wrongdoing.

The voter education program was extensive and multifaceted. It was carried out through the electronic and print media, pamphlets, posters, stickers, and discussions with organized groups. Women and young voters were targeted as groups needing extra attention. As an innovation, a drama presentation woven around unacceptable election practices was shown several times on national television in English and in many of the local languages, and it was performed live for the public in some of the principal towns. For persons living in the remote parts of the country who were unlikely to benefit from the pamphlets or the print and electronic media programs because of illiteracy or lack of access, the EC mounted a special awareness campaign whereby trained personnel went to their locations, took them through the voting procedure at meetings specifically organized for the purpose, and held discussions with them on the election process in general.

Knowing that it could not reach everybody effectively by itself, the EC solicited the assistance of religious groups and various nongovernmental and public interest organizations in expanding its public education effort. They were supplied with carefully prepared materials to ensure accuracy of content. The enthusiasm with which the groups and organizations responded indicated widespread civic society interest and willingness to participate in the democratization effort.

## Other Reforms

On the assumption that people's perceptions and suspicions form part of the electoral landscape and need to be confronted as reality, the EC introduced other innovations into the election process. Among them were transparent ballot boxes and cardboard voting screens. These were intended to forestall allegations of stuffing ballot boxes before voting and ballot dumping during voting—allegations made in connection with the 1992 elections by losing candidates and widely believed by the general public. A transparent ballot box that was not empty on arrival at the polling station would be self-evident. On the other hand, a cardboard screen placed on top of a table in full public view of the voter preserved the secrecy of the ballot while enhancing the chances of detecting the introduction of any extra ballot papers concealed on a voter's person.

The electoral reforms were helped greatly by generous financial and technical support received from international donors. This enabled the commission to build, in a substantial way, its material and manpower capacity toward the delivery of fair elections. For example, the U.S. government provided $6.5 million for purchasing election materials and equipment, providing technical assistance for registration of voters, and paying some of the expenses on the elections; Denmark provided $3 million for purchasing transparent ballot boxes, training registration staff, exhibition staff, polling staff, and political party agents, and conducting voter education; and Britain gave $0.8 million for voter registration forms and equipment for scanning data on registration forms.[7]

## Resolving Electoral Conflict

While the logistical improvements noted above and the "smart" pyrotechnics introduced in 1996 had been crucial to the moderation of electoral conflicts and the overall success of the process, they were made possible in large part by the institutional reforms under the 1992 Constitution. Article 43 of the Constitution provided for the establishment of an Electoral Commission of Ghana consisting of seven members—a chairman, two deputy chairmen and four other members—appointed by the president on the advice of the Council of State (a constitutional body of eminent citizens whose duty is to advise the president and other state actors in the discharge of their functions). The major responsibilities and powers of the commission, set out in considerable detail in the constitution and amplified by statute, include the conduct of all referenda and national and local government elections, the de-limitation of electoral constituencies, the compilation and updating of the voter register, voter education, and the registration of political parties. The Constitution also gave the EC the power to make legislation by constitutional instrument for the effective performance of its functions.

With the existence of a body of laws and explicit rules and regulations relating to its functions, the EC was insulated from, and put in a stronger position to lawfully resist, undue external pressures and interference in its work. These laws and rules also provided for the commission both a guide for its actions and a defense from them. And above all, they formed the framework for the resolution of electoral conflict within the limits of the laws of Ghana.

The 1992 Constitution sought to grant the Electoral Commission maximum autonomy to enable it to perform creditably. The EC's autonomy was ensured in three ways: in performing its functions, it "shall not be subject to the direction or control of any person or authority"; once appointed, the three chairpersons (chair and two deputy chairs) have permanent tenure until retirement and are removable only by impeachment; and the commission's expenses are charged directly on the country's consolidated fund.

The independence of the EC was to be demonstrated in a number of important ways in the course of preparing for the 1996 elections. It acted firmly and decisively and stood its ground on a number of test cases where it was convinced that its position was reasonable and lawful. For instance, in connection with the registration of voters, the commission refused to yield to two demands of the ruling party. One related to the issuance of voter ID cards. For lack of adequate resources, the commission decided to issue photo ID cards only to registered voters residing in the country's major towns, where, because of population concentrations and the relative anonymity, voter impersonation is more likely to occur than in the rural areas. Voters in rural areas would be given thumbprint ID cards. The ruling party responded with the position that every registered voter should be given the same form of ID card, whether photo or thumbprint. The commission stuck to its position and issued both photo and thumbprint ID cards. The ruling party's second demand was to extend the registration period from fifteen to thirty days. Again, the commission refused, arguing that the period afforded persons who really wanted to register ample opportunity to do so.

Additionally, the commission was able to resolve some conflicts simply by explaining the reasons for its actions or indicating the sources of its authority. For example, when it became apparent that there was agitation for the government to set the date for the presidential election, the EC pointed to the constitutional provision empowering it, and not the government, to do so. When the commission refused to allow an alliance formed by two parties to use one symbol to contest the elections, it referred to the law requiring a candidate to use the symbol of his or her political party. When the commission refused to permit party executives to withdraw duly nominated candidates of their party, it said the law gave the right of withdrawal only to the candidate himself or herself.

However, the EC did not rely on its constitutional powers alone to manage electoral conflicts. Perhaps the most important mechanism for managing distrust of the EC by the opposition parties and among the various political parties was the innovative Inter-Party Advisory Committee (IPAC), formed in 1994 by the commission. IPAC brought representatives of the political parties and the election authority together in regular meetings to discuss preparations for the elections. It opened a line of communication and dialogue between the political parties and the election authority and among the parties themselves. IPAC operated under clear guidelines: a meeting would be held at least once a month; every registered political party was free to send representatives; meetings would be closed to the public and the press to facilitate the frank exchange of views; the parties would bring their concerns to the EC for discussion; the EC would bring its election plans and programs to the IPAC for comment and advice; and as a nonstatutory, purely advisory body, IPAC's decisions would not be binding on the EC, which, in accordance with the country's constitution, would have the final word on how elections were to be administered.

Even though it was purely advisory, IPAC played a crucial role in building consensus on the election process and reforms for use in the 1996 elections. In most instances, if what IPAC wanted done was practicable, cost-effective, and not in conflict with the election law, the EC adopted it. In all, the open avenue for dialogue and active collaboration provided by IPAC proved mutually beneficial to the EC and the political parties and helped to clear misunderstandings and defuse tensions about the election process. Indeed, IPAC became so successful as a forum for resolving electoral conflict that it was replicated in the regions and districts.

Another factor in the moderation of electoral conflict, and especially in minimizing disputes over the results of the poll, was the strong involvement of civic bodies and key elements of civil society in the polling process. Prominent national organizations such as the Christian Council of Churches/Catholic Secretariat and civic groups such as the Ghana Legal Literacy Resource Foundation embarked on political/voter education campaigns, in conjunction with statutory bodies such as the National Commission on Civic Education and the EC as well as the political parties. Two society-based domestic poll-watching groups were formed—Ghana Alert and the Network of Domestic Election Observers (NEDEO). These groups helped to mobilize most of the available domestic resources for nongovernmental election monitoring. They selected suitable personnel from their organizations for training and deployment as monitors; they placed communication, transport, and other equipment at the disposal of the network; and they established a machinery for monitoring the pre-election environment. Between NEDEO and Ghana Alert, the domestic poll-watching groups trained more than 4,200 personnel nationwide and deployed them to all 200 constituencies of the country and some 3,100 polling stations representing more than 21 percent of all polling stations and covering most of the conflict-prone parts of the country.

Preparations by the domestic bodies to monitor the elections began in July 1996, four months before the elections. Thus, they were well placed to observe and report on developments before, during, and after voting. The involvement of local monitors, who had a better knowledge of the local scene than most external observers and, especially, an ability to conduct at least a crude parallel vote count and to assist in efforts to check claims of fraud, enhanced the transparency of the election process and boosted public confidence in the outcomes of those elections. The support and encouragement of the EC was a significant factor in the success of the independent domestic poll-watching groups. But it was also helpful to the EC, because the domestic bodies were also in a position to vouch for the EC's integrity. Indeed, the presence of domestic election observer organizations provided an opportunity for the EC to demonstrate its independence from the ruling party as the latter and its agents expressed strong opposition to the domestic groups and put pressure on the EC to deny accreditation.

That the EC had gone to extraordinary lengths in its efforts to institutionalize transparency and fairness in the election process is, at least in part, a reflection of the severe polarization in Ghanaian politics. The EC's efforts in this regard must also be seen against a background of deep and widespread suspicion among large sections of the public, and especially the opposition parties, that the body was inherently biased in favor of the Rawlings government. To be sure, some of the suspicions reflect paranoia on the part of the Ghanaian opposition. But they derive also from the fact that the EC is basically a holdover from the pre-constitutional-rule INEC; its chairman (Afari-Gyan) had been INEC's deputy chairman, and its deputy chairman (David Kanga) was a commissioner of INEC. In addition, and as noted above, INEC was widely perceived, rightly or wrongly to have been complicit in the "rigging" of the November 1992 transition election in favor of the NDC.

An INEC that was hastily established to administer a "snap" election, and whose commissioners the quasi-military Rawlings government had appointed rather unilaterally without consulting the opposition, was bound to be regarded with a great deal of skepticism. Moreover, INEC itself was grafted onto the National Commission on Democracy (NCD), the body that had been created by a decree of the Provisional National Defense Council as part of the Rawlings populist revolution (to replace the existing Electoral Commission). That the efforts of the NCD had gone mainly into canvassing the government's position against liberal democracy in general and multiparty and competitive elections in particular, and that it had provided employment to cadres of the revolution returning home from training in Eastern bloc countries in the mid- to late 1980s, could not escape the notice of the articulate public.

It is not surprising, therefore, that suspicions of pro-government bias and inadequate autonomy linger, notwithstanding the measures introduced by the EC to increase transparency in the electoral process and to foster consultation with the political parties. Clearly, the composition of the EC has yet to inspire bipartisan credibility and maximum assurance of the independence of that body—even though members of the present commission have been appointed by the president in consultation with the council of state, and their security of tenure is guaranteed by the commission.

As described earlier, individuals and parties aggrieved by the actions of the EC can go to the courts to seek relief. Ghana's election law permits not only political parties and election candidates but also practically any elector to bring a court action against the EC. So far, court cases instituted against the commission fall into the following categories: individual citizens questioning the adequacy of preparations for elections; political parties questioning the commission's authority for taking certain measures; and losing candidates disputing election results. With the singular exception of a Constituency Boundaries Tribunal, which the Constitution proposes that the Chief Justice set up from time to time to deal with delimitation grievances, the country's general courts system constitutes the framework for the resolution conflicts that arise over the performance of the Commission's functions.

However, this generalized conflict resolution mechanism has not lent itself to the speedy resolution of electoral conflict usually associated with specialized electoral tribunals. Election cases tend to drag on, seemingly interminably, in part because of the appellate system and in part because there is no codified election case law or clear legal principles readily available to guide judges in the resolution of electoral conflict. For instance, a case in an Accra constituency in which one of the contestants is seeking to overturn the declaration of the results of the December 7 polls in his favor has been dragging on—despite the fact that the EC has admitted it made a mistake in tallying the results and also that the ballot box for one polling station in that constituency was not counted. It is beginning to appear that once election results are declared, reversal is most unlikely, especially where reversal is adverse for the ruling party. That would seem to create an incentive to rig the initial declaration of election results in one's favor.

The idea of election observation by nonpartisan external and domestic bodies seems to have been established in the 1996 polls. However, its sustained practice cannot be taken for granted. Domestic civil society is certainly high on enthusiasm and desire to play an active role in electoral processes. The existing human resource base for civic work is somewhat adequate. But it is woefully lacking in organizational capacity and financial resources. While the 1996 experience generated considerable capacity-building, the domestic poll-watching groups had depended heavily on external agencies for resources to implement their programs and resist governmental efforts to scuttle their initiatives. Financial and moral support from external donors, especially the National Democratic Institute and the U.S. Agency for International Development Mission in Ghana, had been crucial to the work and eventual success of NEDEO. For all its potential as a "permanent" nonpartisan domestic poll watcher and a facilitator of mediation between the EC and political parties and among the parties, NEDEO has gone defunct after the 1996 elections—for want of funding.

### Conclusions

In the preparations leading up to the 1996 elections, the Electoral Commission of Ghana undertook several electoral reforms that contributed to the delivery of fair elections and the general acceptance of the results. In its reform program, the EC sought to do well the things for which it was responsible as an election authority, respond effectively to concerns about the electoral system, and create a transparent and verifiable election process that facilitates the resolution of electoral conflict. It sought to achieve transparency and accountability not only through electoral arrangements but also through dialogue and partnership with the political parties.

It recognized that as the primary stakeholders in democratic elections, political parties have a role to play in the administration of elections, and that in the case of the newly emerging democracies, their preparations for and involvement in the implementation of electoral programs would seem to be critical.

Constant dialogue between an election authority and the political parties helped to lessen unnecessary tensions and apprehensions and to keep complaints to a minimum. However, a recomposition of the commission on the basis of bipartisan consultation and agreement, or the inclusion of representatives of identifiable political and social forces (along the lines of Benin's election authority), may be considered as a way of removing the lingering credibility problems of the EC.

The autonomy and material and manpower capacity of an election authority is crucial to institutional accountability in election administration. The election authority must be entirely free to take actions in accordance with law. Fortunately, there is a broad consensus in Ghana on the need for a truly independent election body. As a result, as long as the EC acts within the law, people are disposed to accept its authority. In this regard, it helped a great deal that the election body could always refer to the constitution, a law, or a regulation to buttress its action in times of conflict. Good election rules, impartially applied by competent election officials, helped to steer the election authority away from trouble. Insofar as adjudication is concerned, it is to be hoped that, out of the several election-related cases coming before the courts, there will emerge a body of case law and clear principles for the resolution of electoral conflict.

Reforming the election administration process to achieve a more congenial election environment should be a continuing, and not a one-shot, activity. For example, the problems of funding of political parties to achieve a more level playing field, equal party access to the media, and real or perceived excessive exploitation of incumbency need to be addressed. Indeed, elections form only a part of a democratic dispensation. The democratization of the general environment to create a democratic culture in support of democratic elections remains imperative.

# 7

# RACE, ETHNICITY, AND VOTING BEHAVIOR
## Lessons from South Africa

Robert B. Mattes and Amanda Gouws

Perhaps the central challenge to establishing genuine competitive democracy in societies divided by race, language, or religion is the often-observed tendency for the "segments" of those societies to give large proportions of their votes to political parties associated with those segments (Horowitz 1985, 1991; Rabushka and Shepsle 1972; Lijphart 1977). Samuel P. Huntington has argued that democratization often "promotes communalism and ethnic conflict" because enduring communal identities offer an easy and tempting basis on which candidates and parties may mobilize support (Huntington 1996b). Election results such as these that consistently resemble a "census" of a society are dangerous to democracy.[1] According to Seymour M. Lipset (1960:12–13),

> A stable democracy requires a situation in which all the major political parties include supporters from many segments of the population. A system in which the support of different parties corresponds too closely to basic social divisions cannot continue on a democratic basis, for it reflects a state of conflict so intense and clear-cut as to rule out compromise. Where parties are cut off from gaining support among a major stratum, they lose a major reason for compromise.

Because political parties fail to span the politically relevant societal cleavages, they lose their ability to mitigate conflict and broker demands. Numerically smaller groups come to feel they have no hope of ever winning an election, and face a future as a permanent minority. Perhaps more important, smaller groups come to feel they have no influence between elections because the governing party (with a secure support base in its numerically greater segment) does not have to anticipate the reactions of voters as it makes public policy and is, therefore, unaccountable to the electorate as a whole. Smaller groups, then, quickly learn to question the legitimacy of elections. Elections in particular, and democracy in general, cease to be exercises in conflict management. Rather, they may ironically become the chief catalyst of conflict.

Viewing elections as "censuses" offers a useful description of the central problem confronting democracy in divided societies. In his 1985 book *Ethnic Groups in Conflict,* Donald Horowitz used the "census" analogy as a central part of his explanation of such electoral outcomes, an explanation that has had a powerful influence on analysts of divided societies, as well as on many politicians within those societies. This has certainly been true of South Africa, where a wide range of domestic political analysts, as well as prominent visiting observers such as Giovanni Sartori, have explained the results of its historic founding 1994 election as an "ethnic" or a "racial census."[2]

Horowitz argued that census-like electoral outcomes are the result of "ascriptive voting"—voting determined by (or at least largely shaped by) birth or descent, rather than by a conscious consideration of party programs or incumbent performance. Voters do not register choice, but identity. Seen from this perspective, election events become elections only in the most formal sense. Election results reflect demographic distributions, or ethnic or racial censuses, rather than popular preferences. And election campaigns cease to fulfill the ideal role as debates about ideas and performance and begin to be exercises solely in ethnic mobilization. If democracy requires a high degree of electoral indeterminacy and uncertainty (Przeworski 1991), ascriptive voting is antithetical to the "free electoral choice" necessary for such uncertainty.

We contend, however, that while the "census" image may provide a useful description of elections in divided societies, as an explanation of individual voting behavior in such cases, census theory suffers from a range of methodological and theoretical problems. This chapter examines this explanation in the case of South Africa's historic election of 1994.

Two concepts central to the census theory of voting behavior are "ethnic parties" and "ethnic voters." Horowitz defined ethnic parties (EPs) as those that embrace the demands of some ethnic group and identify with its cause. More specifically, EPs are those that derive an "overwhelming" proportion of support from one ethnic group, or cluster of groups, to the exclusion of others (Horowitz 1985: 295). Horowitz defined ethnic voting as occurring when a defined group overwhelmingly gives its votes to a party identified with that group. Under conditions of such "ascriptive predictability," he said, voters go to the "polls to register their affiliation," and "choice is preempted by birth." (1985: 319–24). Ethnic voters (EVs) are those people who "choose, in effect, not to choose but to give their vote predictably on an ethnic basis to an ethnically defined party." And, because ethnic voters "put voters of the other group who do choose among parties at a collective disadvantage," ethnic votes tend to drive out nonethnic votes (1985: 346). The clear implication is that communal solidarity pressures supersede other voter concerns, so that voters may actually vote against their interests, or at least vote irrespective of them.

In his analysis of South Africa's first election with a full franchise (including the black majority) in 1994, prominent South African political analyst Lawrence Schlemmer argued:

> To a substantial degree the outcome was not based on the kind of pragmatic voter concerns for which parties can be held accountable. This is not to say that such specific interests did not feature at all but that they were obscured by muscular mobilisation and control of territory and by some very vague, pervasive and powerful symbolic features. . . . perhaps the greatest problem for democratic development is the *artificial* polarisation between Africans (excluding rural Zulus) who overwhelmingly support the ANC, and whites who support the NP very substantially and who generally would appear to have supported almost any party except the ANC (and the PAC). Africans and whites comprise voters with a wide diversity of pragmatic interests, some of which overlap. Yet the election outcome, as far as whites and non-Zulu

Africans were concerned, was uncomfortably close to being a *racial census* [Schlemmer 1994: 197, first emphasis added].

### Problems with the Census Explanation

One relatively minor problem is the lack of precision, especially with regard to the word "overwhelmingly." Does a group have to give two-thirds, three-fourths, or virtually all of its votes to a party to qualify as ethnic voters? But again, this is a small quibble. A second problem with the concepts of EPs and EVs is that they are after the fact. We can only determine an ethnic party or an ethnic voter by the election result (with the exception of the other definition of an EP as one that embraces group demands or identifies with its cause). Should there not be a way to define these concepts so that predictions before an election can be tested against the election result? The importance of this matter was accentuated by the South African example. As late as 1992, one might have reasonably expected a racial census outcome operating along a white versus nonwhite axis with Indian and coloured voters lining up with African voters against their former oppressors. However, once pre-election polls began to indicate, and as the election confirmed, that coloured and Indian voters would overwhelmingly back the governing National Party (NP), the party that had created and implemented apartheid, analysts still explained the results as a racial census, only now along a black versus nonblack axis.[3] After-the-fact analyses noted that whites voted white and blacks voted black (for the most part). Coloured support for the formerly white NP was explained as a reflection of common cultural affinity between whites and coloureds centered around the Afrikaans language and membership in the family of Dutch Reformed churches.[4]

The third, and perhaps the greatest, drawback of census theory (at least with regard to *Ethnic Groups in Conflict*) derives from the lack of appropriate data. First of all, Horowitz focused almost exclusively on aggregate district or regional voting returns in Guyana, Trinidad, Congo, Ghana, and India to substantiate the existence of ethnic voting. Ethnic voting was determined by the pattern by which that group distributed its vote. Thus, census theory committed a significant ecological fallacy by using group-level voting patterns to infer individual-level motivations. Second, where we have had individual-level data, we usually have not had any measure of individual motivations. In his analysis, for example, Horowitz did cite some survey data, but only to examine the relationship of ethnic identity and vote choice.

But neither aggregate data nor demographic background variables (such as language, race, or religion) give us any usable information by which to differentiate an ethnic vote (awarded to a party because of cultural affinity or a desire to express ethnic solidarity) and a nonethnic vote for the same party based on a conscious consideration of competing parties and candidates. Surely an ethnic vote must be intended as such ("choose, in effect, not to choose"), but we almost always lack data on motivation.

We are told that a group giving 90 percent of its vote to one party is comprised of ethnic voters, but that one which distributes its votes, say 55 to 45 percent between two parties, is not. However, it is a mistake to take a high correlation of ethnicity and voting returns as evidence of a "high rate of ethnic voting." Even if the relationship were much lower, it would not necessarily mean that the incidence of ethnic voting was any lesser (or any greater). In other words, there is no necessary relationship between the size of the correlation between ethnicity and the vote and the existence or absence of ethnically motivated voting. Ethnically motivated votes might conceivably exist in equal proportions of the 55 to 45 percent split and the 90 to 10 percent split. The behavior of "white" and "Afrikaner" voters in the South African election was a very good case in point. As a group, they both distributed their votes in significant proportions across at least four different parties, yet there is a fairly good possibility of a concentration of ethnically based voting within the smaller share given to the Freedom Front (the champion of an Afrikaner homeland).

In many respects, the lack of individual data is not the fairest criticism. Given the violent and often underdeveloped nature of most divided societies, it is likely that few systematic surveys have been done to examine individual attitudes. The important point, however, is that our understanding of electoral politics in divided societies may be obscured for lack of individual-level survey data.

Yet even where survey techniques have been employed, our understanding of elections in divided societies may still be hindered by a fourth problem: the reliance on older forms of the "sociological" approach to voting theory, which sees the vote as the product of social characteristics, conditions, or influences (Lazarfeld, Berelson, and Gaudet 1948). Through its emphasis on group pressures, the census explanation implicitly shares many of the principal tenets of the sociological model of voting. Group membership and loyalties are seen to determine, or at least shape, the vote by providing important reference points and by pressuring people to respond to political stimuli in common ways.

Analysts loosely anchored in the sociological approach often fail to measure specific attitudes and remain content with measuring various demographic and economic factors. However, identifying the covariance of demographic factors with voting patterns does not constitute a satisfactory social scientific explanation of individual behavior and motivation. Quite simply, correlation does not equal causation. As Christopher Achen has argued, correlations between demographic factors and the vote do not explain the vote; rather, they themselves need to be explained. "Occupying a particular social niche may help us guess the voter's experiences and beliefs, but they are not themselves explanatory." "Demographics are clues, not hypotheses." Instead, we need to ask, "what is it about a given demographic factor that makes different voters vote differently" (Achen 1992: 206, 209)?

However, it is important to note that analysts using census theory also depart significantly from the sociological approach in a few important ways. Analysts of divided societies (such as Horowitz, Alvin Rabushka, and Kenneth Shepsle) and South African political analysts (such as Schlemmer, R. W. Johnson, Hermann Giliomee, and David Welsh) see group-based voting as a statement of identity, loyalty and solidarity, or even as a result of group pressures for political conformity. The clear implication is that such a high correlation of the vote and group membership would not exist if voters followed their true interests.

In contrast, the political sociologists have cited far different reasons for a high correlation of group identity and the vote. While they have seen one's social group as an important factor, they have offered very different explanations for this. One variant sees group influence operating not so much through group pressure as through the socializing effects of repeated interaction and reinforcement. Another variant sees the use of group opinion as a reference point for a fairly rational process of utilizing cues or informational shortcuts (Dalton 1988: 152). The covariance of group identity and political opinion arises because individual positions in a social structure often indicate individual values and beliefs. Social structure, therefore, becomes an indirect measure or proxy of attitudinal difference (Dalton 1988). Thus, political sociologists have seen "group-based" votes as instrumental acts to support the party that will best maximize group interest. In contrast, census theorists see group-based votes as expressions of identity, and expressions that often contradict individual interests (Lipset 1960: 239). But it is clear that a high correlation of the key cleavage variable and the vote is not necessarily the result of nonrational or primordial motivations. There are several possible alternative explanations for a high correlation of group membership and the vote besides the one advanced by census theory.

### Understanding the South African Voter

A fuller understanding of voting in South Africa (and other divided societies) requires individual-level data. But more important, it requires us to go beyond the sociological approach and make use of key insights from both the "social psychological" (Campbell, Miller, Converse, and Stokes 1960) and the "economic" or "rational choice" approaches to voting (Downs 1957; Key 1966). First of all, this means that we need to consider the role of individual interest. Especially in a divided society like South Africa, it is likely that issues and interests run parallel to factors such as race or ethnicity. Given that the very essence of apartheid meant that life chances differed fundamentally according to race, individual interests have been structured largely along racial lines. Thus, race may provide a useful informational shortcut that tells voters where their interests lie. It is a useful thought experiment to consider whether predicted South African voting patterns would differ markedly from the actual 1994 results if all voters were assumed to operate according to naked economic self-interest.

This theoretical shift also requires us to locate the prime influences on individual voting decisions at a point closer in both time and space to the actual act of voting—influences that intervene between demographic background characteristics and the vote. This means that we should focus not so much on objective measures of interest as on voters' values and perceptions of their interests and on how various parties, candidates, and incumbents may serve those interests. This allows us to see the vote as a more rational act based on voters' understandings of the information at hand. Voter rationality does not imply omniscience or civic altruism. According to Achen, rationality merely assumes that "Voters do not ignore the information they have, do not fabricate information they do not have, and do not choose what they do not want. Thus, the voters need be neither geniuses nor saints. They are required only to do the best with the information they have" (Achen 1992: 198).

Finally, we also need to retain key insights from what the sociological approach and cognitive psychology have taught us about how people process information. Perceptions of reality are shaped by the social context in which one receives, filters, and interprets information. One of the effects of the apartheid policy of Group Areas is that the information networks of vast majorities of black, white, coloured, or Indian voters have been contained for the greatest part wholly within particular cultural milieus, each of which was fairly consistent internally and offered few cross-pressures. Voters' information about their interests and past events (such as apartheid, the struggle against apartheid, the repeal of apartheid, and the transition to democracy) is likely to have been received through screens, or informational gatekeepers, that ran parallel to race. Thus, voters from different racial groups and different ethnic communities are likely to have seen starkly different political worlds when they went to the polls in 1994.

With one of the highest levels of income inequality in the world, white voters proceeded from a material base of first world affluence, far outstripping that of black voters. Moreover, their understandings of those interests and the threats to them, as well as of recent political performance, had been shaped by the particular interpretations of Christian National Education, the South African Broadcasting Company, the conservative Afrikaans *Nasionale Pers* (National Press), or the liberal English print media.

While attempting to characterize the world view of any group is fraught with problems, it seems fairly certain that most whites would have had at least a fairly conservative view of political change, seeing moves toward racial equality as a threat to their interests. For almost all whites, media depictions of the principal proponents of the struggle against apartheid, the African National Congress (ANC) and the Pan-Africanist Congress (PAC), would have been uniformly negative. They would have been seen as communist-aligned, if not wholly communist, organizations who favored radical redistribution of wealth away from whites, and who were bent on achieving black domination through a combination of international sanctions and a terrorist war of violence. On the other hand, the Inkatha Freedom Party (IFP), the nominally governing party of the KwaZulu homeland, was portrayed as more capitalist, with a conservative interest in maintaining traditional values, and thus more likely to cooperate and engage in negotiations with the government.

For most whites, especially Afrikaners, the governing National Party was able to portray itself through the state media and the aligned Afrikaans press as the only party able to safeguard whites' interests and values, resist attempts at a violent takeover by communist-aligned black power proponents, and yet simultaneously steer the country toward a new political dispensation. However, for the most conservative Afrikaners who still favored "grand apartheid" and the attempt to banish blacks to "independent national states," the most appropriate defender of their values and interests in the election would have been the Freedom Front (FF). Formed only weeks before the election by members of the election-boycotting Conservative Party (CP), the FF was the electoral expression of those Afrikaners who had broken away from the NP in 1983 in reaction to the government's attempts to reform grand apartheid through a cooptive form of racial consociationalism.

Relatively liberal English-speaking whites, receiving political information through the state-run broadcast media but also through the more liberal and capitalist English press, would certainly not have been sympathetic to black liberation organizations. Yet they would have been more critical of government excesses and violations of individual rights, especially the repressive security legislation of the 1980s. Not surprisingly, the support base of the liberal parliamentary opposition parties (of which the Democratic Party [DP] was the latest heir) historically had been predominantly English-speaking.

Black voters, on the other hand, began from an entirely different material base, characterized by high levels of unemployment, poverty, and illiteracy, and by relatively little access to quality health care or education. Politically, they had been deprived of rights through the well-known matrix of laws, customs, and regulations known as the apartheid system. Given such desperate conditions, the necessity of radical (and even violent) political change was almost certainly widely accepted. Black voters received an understanding of their interests and of recent political performance through informational gatekeepers such as trade unions, civic associations, street committees, and the radical or progressive print media. Given this context, the NP obviously bore the heavy legacy of apartheid and forty years of legalized oppression. While President F. W. de Klerk had undertaken a radical departure in February 1990 by unbanning the liberation organizations and releasing Nelsen Mandela from prison, the succeeding four years saw escalating violence in black townships. The government and its security forces were widely suspected by the black media and informational network of fomenting this violence, thus nullifying any potential positive spin-offs from the earlier moves.

In sharp contrast, the exiled ANC and PAC both enjoyed long histories as the preeminent organizations fighting for black liberation. The ANC, however, had been far more successful than the PAC in establishing a public reputation for fighting and winning the struggle against apartheid. It was able to maintain a continued physical presence in black townships and strong links with its internal allies such as the United Democratic Front and allied labor unions in a campaign designed to make the townships ungovernable. It also sustained a campaign of widely publicized bombings of "hard" military and security targets as well as "softer" targets throughout the 1980s. In contrast, the PAC was able to establish a credible internal military presence only after 1990, and it began hitting its targets (largely white farmers and a white church that was subjected to a highly publicized bombing) only after constitutional negotiations were well under way.

Finally, while those people assigned by apartheid into the coloured or Indian racial groups had also been the subject of severe state oppression and were economically much worse off than whites, they had also been relatively advantaged in comparison with blacks. The coloured community of the western portion of the Cape Province had particularly benefited from the government's coloured labour preference policy. And while the limited self-government over "own affairs" through the Tricameral Parliament (created by the government's 1983 reform constitution) hardly amounted to real democracy, the patronage provided by this cooptive strategy did result in some considerable material advancements, especially in the coloured community. Thus, while they had suffered considerably at the hands of the NP, they had also witnessed some gradual progress as a result of government reforms. Moreover, De Klerk's bold moves of 1990, and the subsequent removal of racist legislation, had signaled the possibility of a fundamentally changed NP. De Klerk helped to cement this image by going to great lengths to apologize to coloured audiences for apartheid (something he never did in front of black audiences—though, to be fair, grassroots intolerance in black townships never presented him with many opportunities).

Coloured and Indian voters' long-standing informational links to white-run state broadcasters and press meant that they had been supplied over the previous decade with a thoroughly negative view of the ANC as a communist, terrorist organization bent on black domination whose strategies had introduced considerable violence into these communities. Moreover, their relative economic advantages and the limited political and economic gains of the 1980s meant that these voters saw the type of radical and violent change advocated by the ANC or the PAC as much less of a necessity than it was for black voters. By the time of the 1994 election, these communities were relatively more modernized, more urbanized, better housed, and better educated, and far more ready to compete for economic advancement, than were black South Africans. Thus, while both of these relatively conservative communities stood to gain considerably from the removal of apartheid, they also perceived a significant political and economic threat from the numerically much larger and much poorer black majority represented by the ANC.

## Analysis

While the outcome of South Africa's first election open to all South Africans may have descriptively resembled an ethnic or a racial census, census theory does not adequately explain the reasons for this outcome. In contrast to the census approach, which uses aggregate voting data or individual survey data to examine the correlation of ascribed identity and voting behavior, we use data from a nationally representative post-election survey to examine the degree to which political preferences were actually driven by identity-related motivations.[5] Moreover, we focus not on actual voting day behavior, but on partisan identification. Our conceptualization of partisan support differs fundamentally from the census approach, which sees party support in divided societies as relatively fixed and is based on identity rather than evaluations of performance. Drawing on the work of *The American Voter,* but also on important modifications made by V. O. Key (1966) and Christopher Achen (1992), we conceptualize partisan identification as a relatively longer-term "standing decision," which may differ from the short-term voting decision. This decision is based partly on early socializing experiences, but also on evolving evaluations of party performance (evaluations which themselves are shaped by pre-existing identification as well as informational screens).

## Ascribed Identity and the Vote

We begin by examining the degree to which the outcome of South Africa's first election actually resembled an ethnic or a racial census. We turn first to Horowitz's concept of ethnic or racial parties. As mentioned earlier, one problem with Horowitz's operationalization was its lack of specification of "overwhelming": thus, we use Richard Rose and Derek Urwin's criteria for stating that a party is based on a social group, that at least two-thirds of supporters must share a given characteristic (Rose and Urwin 1969). Consistent with Horowitz's expectations, party support does correlate strongly with ascribed identity, although there are important exceptions.

Five of the parties that eventually won parliamentary seats could be labeled "racial parties" if we use the two-thirds criterion. The ANC, the IFP, and the PAC were "black" parties (the IFP has the highest proportion of white supporters—11.8 percent). The FF and the DP were "white." In this regard, Horowitz's admonition against being misled by multiethnic candidate slates or campaign platforms is affirmed. Despite the protestations and the best intentions of many in the ANC, it had a highly racial support base. Ironically, only the NP, the progenitor of apartheid, had a nonracial support base nationally. Just over one-half of its identifiers were white, 40 percent were coloured and Indian, and 8.7 percent were black. (See table 7-1.)

However, many have argued that the racial cleavages of apartheid artificially conceal a much more real set of divisions revolving around ethnicity, tribalism, and nationality, divisions that will become more important as the memory of apartheid recedes (Horowitz 1991; Lijphart 1985). A good indicator of ethnicity (as distinct from race) is home language. According to the two-thirds criterion, the most ethnically based parties are the IFP, the FF, and, perhaps surprisingly, the liberal DP. The IFP derives 85.7 percent of its support from Zulu-speakers. Also of interest, it gets three quarters of its white support from English-speakers as opposed to Afrikaans-speakers (although this is based on a very small number of voters in our sample). While the FF gets 100 percent of its support from whites, it gets 82.9 percent of its support from white

**Table 7-1.** Racial Breakdown of Party Support Bases

|  | ANC | NP | IFP | FF | DP | PAC | Independent | Total |
|---|---|---|---|---|---|---|---|---|
| Black | 94.3 | 7.8 | 88.1 | — | 3.1 | 93.0 | 68.7 | 72.2 |
| White | 0.2 | 52.2 | 11.8 | 100.0 | 87.5 | — | 24.1 | 16.2 |
| Coloured | 4.3 | 31.1 | 0.3 | — | 9.4 | 6.1 | 6.0 | 8.8 |
| Indian | 1.0 | 8.9 | — | — | — | — | 1.2 | 2.8 |
|  | 100.0 | 100.0 | 100.0 | 100.0 | 100.0 | 100.0 | 100.0 | 100.0 |

**Table 7-2.** Ethnic Breakdown of Party Support Bases (Home Language)

|  | ANC | NP | IFP | FF | DP | PAC | Independent | Total |
|---|---|---|---|---|---|---|---|---|
| Zulu | 22.4 | 1.4 | 85.7 | — | 3.1 | 25.0 | 26.0 | 23.0 |
| Afrikaans | 3.8 | 59.9 | 3.0 | 82.9 | 28.7 | 4.3 | 14.4 | 16.6 |
| Xhosa | 24.1 | 0.8 | 0.8 | — | — | 28.1 | 1.2 | 15.4 |
| English | 1.7 | 32.0 | 8.7 | 17.0 | 68.8 | — | 18.7 | 10.8 |
| Tswana | 13.1 | 1.7 | — | — | 14.2 | — | 1.2 | 8.4 |
| Sepedi | 10.1 | 1.4 | — | — | — | 12.5 | 4.7 | 7.5 |
| Seswati | 4.0 | 1.1 | 0.8 | — | — | 9.4 | 9.4 | 3.3 |
| Venda | 3.6 | 0.6 | — | — | — | 6.3 | — | 3.1 |
| Shangaan | 4.1 | — | — | — | — | — | — | 3.0 |
|  | 100.0 | 100.0 | 100.0 | 100.0 | 100.0 | 100.0 | 100.0 | 100.0 |

**Table 7-3.** Partisan Identification by Race Group

|  | Black | White | Coloured | Indian | Total | Eta |
|---|---|---|---|---|---|---|
| ANC | 75.2 | 0.8 | 28.4 | 23.9 | 57.6 | 0.59 |
| NP | 1.6 | 48.3 | 53.1 | 47.89 | 15.0 | 0.61 |
| IFP | 6.4 | 3.8 | 0.2 | — | 5.3 | 0.10 |
| FF | — | 13.8 | — | — | 2.2 | 0.34 |
| DP | — | 7.2 | 1.4 | — | 1.3 | 0.23 |
| PAC | 1.8 | — | 0.9 | — | 1.4 | 0.06 |
| Other | 0.6 | 5.9 | 2.1 | 7.9 | 1.8 |  |
| Independent | 11.1 | 15.1 | 11.8 | 19.4 | 12.0 | 0.06 |

*Note:* Columns do not add to 100 percent because "confidential" responses are excluded.

Afrikaans-speakers as opposed to English-speakers. Of the DP's support base, 68.8 percent is English-speaking. The ANC's reputation as a Xhosa political organization clearly is not supported by the composition of its support base. The party draws support from across a range of language groups. The NP comes close to qualifying as an ethnic party: just under 60 percent of its identifiers are Afrikaans-speakers (this is largely because of support from both white and coloured Afrikaans-speakers). (See table 7-2.) One other important point to note is that the parties that had explicitly parochial, ethnic, or racial programs, such as the FF, the IFP and the PAC (as well as other very small parties such as the African Muslim Party, the Islamic Party, the (Indian) Minority Front, and the [Portuguese] Luso-South African Party), did not do well in their intended "target" groups or constituencies.[6]

### Ethnic and Racial Voters?

Now we turn to examine whether, according to Horowitz's concepts, South African voters can be classified as "ethnic" or "racial" voters, looking for defined groups of voters who give "overwhelming support" (two-thirds) to a single party. In terms of party identification, black voters do give more than two-thirds of their support to one party, the ANC (75.2 percent). Moreover, they give 83.4 percent of their support to "black" parties. However, white voters do not overwhelmingly support any one party, and less than half of their support goes to the NP. Only 69.3 percent of white identification is distributed among the NP, the FF, and the DP. Coloured voters are not racial voters, by our definition. Just over half identify with the NP, and almost 30 percent identify with the ANC. Indian voters do not fit into Horowitz's definition either. Just under half identify with the NP, and just over 20 percent with the ANC. (See table 7-3.)

Do any language groups qualify as "ethnic voters"? Xhosas (90 percent), Sotho (86.7 percent) Tswana (89 percent), Shangaan (79 percent), Seswati (69 percent) and Venda (68 percent) give overwhelming proportions of their support to one party, the ANC. Significantly, while the IFP is quite clearly a Zulu-based party, Zulu-speakers cannot be termed to be ethnic voters (in our sample more than half identify with the ANC and a fifth with the IFP).[7] Afrikaans-speakers give more than half their support to the National Party, but give about equal portions to the ANC (13 percent) and to the FF (11 percent). (Again, this high level of ANC support is a result of the inclusion of a substantial number of coloured voters in the Afrikaans category). While the English-speakers give 44 percent to the NP, the rest of their support is quite scattered. (See table 7-4.)

In many respects, the outcome of the South African election resembled a racial census. Yet our brief analysis of the different views that different race groups would likely have of the various parties suggested a range of rational explanations for a very tight correlation between race, ethnicity, and party support. Moreover, even at the level of merely correlating ascribed identity with support patterns, we found some important exceptions. In other words, if we take Horowitz's concepts on their own terms, the concepts of ethnic parties and ethnic voters cannot be consistently applied to the South African situation. In what was widely seen as a classic example of a census election, many defined groups cannot be accurately described as ethnic or racial voters, and several important parties do not qualify as racial or ethnic parties.

### Identity-Related Motivations and Partisan Support

Horowitz conceptually distinguishes between ethnic voters who use their votes to register their affiliation or identity, and nonethnic voters who choose between parties and candidates based on performance or policies. As noted above, we cannot empirically make this distinction by observing aggregate voting returns, or by merely comparing individuals' ascriptive identity and their vote. One way to get at this matter is to examine people's own proffered reasons for their partisan and candidate support. Even if aggregate voting outcomes correlate with ascribed identity, do individual voters connect their group membership with their political support? Are they conscious of their vote as an ethnic or racial vote?

We asked party identifiers, in an open-ended question, why they felt close to their party. The principal, and perhaps surprising, finding here is that the vast majority of South African voters are not

**Table 7-4.** Partisan Identification by Linguistic Groups

| | Zulu | Afrikaans | Xhosa | English | Sotho | Tswana | Sepedi | Seswati | Venda | Shangaan | Eta |
|---|---|---|---|---|---|---|---|---|---|---|---|
| ANC | 56.0 | 13.0 | 90.0 | 8.9 | 86.7 | 89.0 | 77.0 | 69.0 | 68.0 | 79.0 | 0.63 |
| NP | 0.9 | 54.0 | 0.8 | 44.0 | 1.0 | 3.0 | 2.8 | 5.0 | 2.7 | — | 0.61 |
| IFP | 20.0 | 1.0 | 0.3 | 4.2 | 0.5 | — | — | 1.3 | — | — | 0.36 |
| FF | — | 11.1 | — | 3.5 | — | — | — | — | — | — | 0.28 |
| DP | 0.2 | 2.3 | — | 8.5 | — | — | — | — | — | — | 0.29 |
| PAC | 1.4 | 0.3 | 2.4 | — | 2.5 | 1.0 | 2.2 | 3.8 | 2.7 | — | 0.10 |
| Other | 0.2 | 5.3 | — | 3.9 | — | 0.4 | — | — | 9.5 | 2.8 | |
| None | 13.6 | 10.0 | 6.2 | 21.0 | 9.3 | 6.4 | 15.0 | 11.0 | 18.0 | 18.0 | 0.14 |

*Note:* Columns do not add to 100 percent because "confidential" responses are excluded.

conciously aware of race or ethnicity as a primary reason for their party support. Only 10.1 percent of the total sample mentioned race-related reasons as one of the motivations for their support; an additional 3.4 percent mentioned ethnicity. In contrast, ideology was mentioned by 18.1 percent, policies by 15.4 percent, and past or future performance by 27.1 percent. However, once we break down these open-ended reasons for partisan identification according to partisan support, we do see larger concentrations of what might be ethnic or racial voters within certain parties. Of IFP voters, 44.6 percent cited ethnic reasons, 42.2 percent of FF voters mentioned race (and an additional 7.3 percent cited ethnicity), and 29.2 percent of PAC voters mentioned racial reasons. In contrast, the two largest parties depended mainly on factors of policy, performance, and competence (for the NP) and policy, performance, and ideology (for the ANC). (See table 7-5.)

**Table 7-5.** Reasons for Party Identification by Party Support

|  | ANC | NP | IFP | FF | DP | PAC | Total |
|---|---|---|---|---|---|---|---|
| Ideology | 22.3 | 7.6 | 7.8 | 10.9 | 45.0 | 19.8 | 18.3 |
| Past/Present Performance | 20.4 | 19.5 | 7.7 | 2.0 | 15.8 | 15.9 | 18.1 |
| Policy | 15.5 | 12.2 | 4.5 | 38.0 | 7.6 | 27.5 | 15.4 |
| Group/Race | 11.4 | 3.6 | 1.0 | 42.2 | 2.1 | 29.2 | 10.1 |
| Future Performance | 10.5 | 10.1 | 2.3 | 2.0 | 5.8 | — | 9.0 |
| Group/South Africans | 7.7 | 9.4 | 2.9 | 3.4 | 9.1 | 1.4 | 7.2 |
| Don't Like Other Parties | 5.7 | 9.1 | 3.0 | 9.3 | 9.3 | 14.6 | 6.4 |
| Leaders/Candidate | 5.8 | 6.8 | 3.7 | 6.6 | 2.1 | — | 5.8 |
| Competence | 3.0 | 20.8 | 0.7 | — | 3.6 | — | 5.5 |
| Trust/Integrity | 3.5 | 9.9 | 1.9 | 5.5 | 8.8 | — | 4.8 |
| Strength | 3.6 | 5.4 | 2.2 | — | 1.8 | — | 3.9 |
| Party Loyalty | 2.8 | 8.9 | 4.2 | — | 7.3 | 2.8 | 3.8 |
| Group/Ethnicity | 0.1 | 1.1 | 44.6 | 7.3 | — | 2.0 | 3.4 |
| Family Reasons |  |  |  |  |  |  | 1.8 |
| Moral Principles | 0.1 | 0.9 | — | — | — |  | 1.2 |
| Group/Minorities | 0.2 | — | — | — | 3.0 | 2.5 | 0.2 |

The same general patterns emerged when we asked those people who had said they had been attracted to their party by a particular candidate why they found that candidate attractive. In total, 6 percent mentioned race and 4 percent ethnicity. In contrast, 33 percent cited the candidates' performance or achievements, and 22 percent mentioned their competence. When we broke these responses down by specific candidates, we found that Nelson Mandela and F.W. de Klerk largely attracted followers through performance (mentioned by 41 percent and 30 percent of their followers, respectively), ability/competence (18 percent and 31 percent), or integrity/trust (10 percent and 30 percent). In contrast, 45 percent of those attracted to the IFP by Mangosuthu Buthelezi cited his connections to the Zulu-nation or culture, 38 percent of those attracted to the FF by former General Constand Viljoen cited race, and 19 percent of those attracted to the PAC by Clarence Makwetu mentioned race.

When identified through open-ended responses about motivations for party support, we can find voters who fit Horowitz's conception of ethnic voters. They appear to be a relative minority of voters, however, although they seem to comprise a significant portion of the IFP, the FF, and the PAC.

### Reason and Judgment

Perhaps the most important claim of the census explanation of voting in divided societies is that the demands of group solidarity often force people to vote in ways contrary to, or at least irrespective of, their values and their evaluations of political performance. We consider this claim by examining the role of ideology and of retrospective evaluations of political performance.

Did race-based communal interests supersede voters' basic political values? The census model would expect to find a very weak relationship between people's political values and partisan support, arguing that people's partisan loyalties are determined by racial or ethnic identities rather than ideology. One convenient summary statement of ideological beliefs is where people place themselves along a "left/right" continuum, what Russell Dalton (1988: 119) calls an overall political orientation, or a "summary statement" of voters' positions on issues of greatest concern. Even given the limitations imposed by the greatly uneven ability of voters to place themselves on this scale, voter's placement of themselves and the various political parties on this scale reveals some very important patterns (table 7-6). There are clear differences in left/right self-placement by race (at least for those able to place themselves). Blacks are furthest to the left, whites furthest to the right, and coloured and Indian voters near the mean location for all voters.

More important, in accordance with our earlier discussion of the effect of interests, performance, group areas, and racialized information networks, not only did voters of different race groups place themselves at significantly different points along the left/right spectrum, but voters of different races literally "saw" very different worlds when they observed political debate and competition. Taken as a group, black voters saw the PAC and the ANC as fairly similar moderate-left parties, and placed themselves very close to both. Significantly, they placed the IFP to the right of the ideological midpoint and much closer to the DP and the NP. White voters—as a group—placed every political party to the left of themselves (unfortunately, we did not measure perceptions of the FF). Whites had a very different image of the PAC and the ANC than black voters, placing them to the far left, with the PAC almost at the very extreme of the "radical/left-wing" end. Coloured voters placed the PAC and the ANC at far less extreme positions than whites, and placed the NP on the midpoint, with the DP slightly to the right of center (but both relatively more conservative than how whites saw these parties).

Elsewhere (Mattes 1994) we have offered additional evidence to support our thesis, but we believe that the evidence presented here is sufficient to raise doubts about the ethnic census view of South Africa's 1994 election.

## Conclusions

This chapter has presented a series of conceptual flaws with the influential and widely accepted census explanation of individual

**Table 7-6.** Ideological Placement

Scale: 1 (left/radical) to 6 (right/conservative)

| Ideology | Mean Placement | | | | | |
|----------|------|-------|-------|----------|--------|------|
|          | All  | Black | White | Coloured | Indian | Eta  |
| Yourself | 3.20 | 2.87  | 4.03  | 3.04     | 3.35   | 0.34 |
| ANC      | 2.60 | 2.91  | 1.77  | 2.50     | 2.97   | 0.31 |
| NP       | 3.80 | 3.97  | 3.45  | 3.50     | 3.62   | 0.17 |
| IFP      | 3.40 | 3.63  | 3.03  | 3.24     | 3.28   | 0.16 |
| DP       | 3.70 | 3.91  | 3.21  | 3.65     | 3.85   | 0.24 |
| PAC      | 2.40 | 2.89  | 1.28  | 2.51     | 2.48   | 0.45 |

voting behavior in divided societies. And in what has been widely seen as a classic example of an ethnic (or racial) census, we have presented empirical data from the South African case that contradict many of the assumptions and predictions of that theory. Most important, we have seen that political preferences are not widely motivated by group-related attachments. Few people explicitly recognize race or ethnicity as reasons for their partisan identification. Most people viewed the parties they support as inclusive and representative of all South Africans, rather than exclusive and representative of only one group.

Moreover, the supposed impact of group attachment on partisan support in divided societies must be questioned by our finding that those South Africans without, or with less intense, group attachments did not behave differently in any politically or statistically significant ways from those with such attachments. Furthermore, we found that voters' values and performance evaluations played key roles in voter's judgment, and were not set aside out of deference to group attachments to political parties.

It must be noted that we did see important subgroupings of voters who resembled those voters described by Donald Horowitz in *Ethnic Groups In Conflict*. These voters are concentrated within the ranks of followers of the Inkatha Freedom Party, the Freedom Front, and the Pan-Africanist Congress. However, it appears that we could explain the behavior of the great majority of South African voters without placing a huge emphasis on group identity, but rather by utilizing the usual theories of voter behavior developed in apparently "more normal" democracies.

What are the implications for constitutional engineering in divided societies? Most calls for alternative electoral systems and power sharing have been based, if implicitly, on assumptions that voters were tightly sewn in by ethnically based loyalties. While we may question this assumption, we do not pretend to argue that voter loyalties are significantly less fixed. Party identification, even when based on nonethnic reasons, is often very resistant to change. While the ANC does not qualify as a racial or ethnic party, its support is not likely to diminish in the near future. As we have demonstrated, its support base is intimately connected with its success in securing the political freedom of millions of South Africans. That is an accomplishment not easily overwhelmed by inflation, unemployment, lack of housing, or corruption (although those factors may have their effects).

The ANC's huge advantage in terms of longer-term partisan identification means that, under the normal conditions of parliamentary democracy, it is doubtful whether that party will need to form a coalition with any other party for the next few elections. Thus, the ANC may face reduced pressures to anticipate future voter reactions as it makes policy. Yet it is precisely the perceived need to anticipate voter reactions that makes governing parties respond to public opinion and that is the driving force of representative democracy. If South Africa under the ANC had decided to maintain in its final 1996 constitution the proportional power-sharing cabinet of its interim constitution, this might have been a crucial way to retain some measure of competitiveness and electoral uncertainty. A proportional cabinet would have forced the ANC to anticipate not only how its actions would affect its majority/minority status but how any shift in support might alter the crucial distribution of the number and the importance of cabinet seats.

One reason that party identification will probably change slowly is that South African voters will continue to receive and filter information about economic failures or successes through the cognitive

screens of their existing partisan loyalties, as well as through racially structured information networks. Yet political attitudes are
not fixed and may be changed even in the face of strong preexist-
ing biases. It is true that ANC supporters will be more likely to
explain away the continued lack of a house or a job as a reflection
of the recalcitrance of white bureaucrats or selfish capitalists (where
PAC supporters will find fault with the government from the start).
Yet the persistent lack of jobs and shelter (if this indeed happens)
will begin to work at people's cognitive defenses. On the other
hand, NP supporters will be more likely to explain economic growth
as the result of an economic cycle, or careful planning by the
previous De Klerk government, but steady economic improve-
ment will also have an effect.

If no steps are taken to the contrary, voters of different races
will retain very different information networks, if only because of
the sharp separation of communities created by apartheid and the
highly differing racial profiles of the readership of various news-
papers. Thus, movement toward a legitimate and widely accepted
broadcast news media with a common news agenda will be a
crucial step toward creating a common forum for political debate
and criticism. This step would enable continuous debate between
credible party spokesmen and allies in the media and civil society.
Yet political parties also must take significant steps to find people
who enjoy credibility across the racial and partisan divide, especially parties like the PAC, the NP and the DP. In this respect, our
personal experience with party officials in South Africa indicates
that their acceptance of the ethnic census explanation of the election has prevented them from taking hard looks at themselves and
taking significant steps to build credibility.

From this perspective, the very worst thing that could have happened, especially for the opposition parties, would have been to
let the need for reconciliation and consensus drive out the need
for rigorous debate and criticism. Indeed, this was one of the central challenges facing parties in South Africa's interim government
of national unity: how could they criticize decisions of which they
were nominally a part? The NP never solved this dilemma. Once
the NP determined in 1996 that South Africa's Constitutional

Assembly would not retain the power-sharing cabinet past 1999, it made a strategic early departure from government so as to move into opposition and attack the government well in advance of the second election in 1999. This is something that advocates of consociational forms of power sharing need to consider seriously. Because the focus on consensus competes with the real need for serious opposition and debate, political actors are denied the ability to persuade voters, and "census-like" voting patterns may be entrenched rather than ameliorated. Ironically, consociationalism may perpetuate the very divisions in society that it is intended to address.

# ▮ PART IV: Findings

The premise of chapter 8, substantiated by the Appendix, which includes a list of coming elections in Africa, is that regular, popular elections are a permanent feature of political life in Africa. As Glickman pointed out in chapter 2, even dictatorial regimes resort to elections (however managed) to justify their rule. Thus, the question for those seeking to foster democratization *and* conflict management is: How can the meaning and processes of elections in Africa be improved to improve the quality of democratization and to manage conflict?

Chapter 8 provides highlights of the discussion at the June 1995 United States Institute of Peace symposium. As a point of departure, the problems of elections in contemporary Africa are classified and underscored. Moreover, the inherent dilemmas of external parties using elections as a policy instrument to promote conflict management receive special attention. Finally, the essay offers principles for policymakers in governments, international organizations, and nongovernmental organizations on ways to promote elections better as a vehicle for building meaningful democracies and for peacefully managing conflicts.

# 8

# ELECTIONS AND CONFLICT MANAGEMENT IN AFRICA
## Conclusions and Recommendations

Timothy D. Sisk

There is a policy consensus in the international community that elections should be promoted as a necessary ingredient of both democratization and peacemaking. This consensus, although not always explicit and often second-guessed, is revealed in the way that elections—especially free and fair, competitive, multiparty elections—have become a condition in the continued flow of donor assistance and as the crowning event of a peace process after which external parties draw down their engagement. Without fresh elections, at some point and in some manner, neither a transition to democracy nor a transition from war to peace appears possible.

Whether elections signal the end of an entrenched dictatorship and a transition to nascent democracy, as in Malawi, or serve as the way to reconstitute and relegitimize the state after a civil war, as in Mozambique, the international community sees them as critically important, and it promotes them through instruments of external intervention. This reflexive reliance on elections occurs not only in Africa, but in myriad other post-conflict settings around the world. Consider, for example, the emphasis placed in elections in the Dayton, Ohio, agreement that pointed to a way to peace in Bosnia. Elections in Bosnia, held in October 1996, were pursued with vigor by the international community even though there was universal expectation that an election would intensify, not diminish, the polarization of that society along ethnic lines. But the election in Bosnia, like the elections in Africa that have been the subject of analysis in this volume, are promoted even when an environment conducive to democracy does not really exist.

## Elections as an Instrument of Intervention

What lies behind this reliance on elections as a necessary ingredient in democratization and peace-building? Larry Garber of the U.S. Agency for International Development, an experienced U.S. policy practitioner in promoting elections, comments, "It is the only alternative on the table, or the only alternative that is perceived as being on the table, for [Western] policy makers." He continues,

> It's often hard to imagine how a process that appears so inherently divisive, particularly in societies that have been struggling with violence over a period of time, can use an election to resolve their conflicts. Yet in many cases the reality is that diplomats and policymakers and the combatants have no other credible alternative for resolving their conflict than to organize and participate in the electoral process.[1]

Moreover, grassroots democrats on the ground in Africa and elsewhere often want the international community to force political elites to legitimate their rule through the ballot box, and they often want the United States, in particular, to be engaged. Vivian Derryck, erstwhile president of the African-American Institute, an organization that has been actively involved in democracy-building in Africa, argues that "those Africans that we deal with want us to be there." Elections not only are promoted from without, but are demanded by opposition groups from within.

A principal conclusion emanating from the analysis in this volume is that this reflexive turn to elections by the international community, despite all the problems associated with them, has considerable merit. As a tool of international intervention, elections can be a very robust and effective instrument. Elections can contribute to democratization and to ameliorating and managing conflict under appropriate circumstances. For the international community, seeking to intervene to promote, as UN Secretary General Boutros Boutros-Ghali commented (1992), "mechanisms for the institutionalization of peace," elections can serve many roles simultaneously.

Elections can legitimate democratization moves or a peace process, reaffirming the paramount role of the new rules of the political game. When the international community engages to monitor or verify an election, as Derryck notes, "We are confirming and affirming that they are just and valid in this particular instance." Despite all of their inherent difficulties, elections are critical to legitimate political change because there is simply no more credible alternative.

Elections can also serve to broaden the base of participation and validate the right of peaceful opposition to incumbent regimes; indeed, it is likely that opposition parties are the most vocal proponents of testing a government's mandate at the polls. As Harvey Glickman notes in this volume, elections can also serve to arbitrate, often in a very subtle manner, the underlying disputes in conflict, helping to create a culture where parties turn to institutions to resolve differences, rather than to violence.

The elections process can serve as a vehicle for deeper and longer-lasting international intervention in helping manage deadly internal conflicts. Ideally, intervention can serve to create a long-term capacity for continued democracy, so that a reliance on elections becomes simply a start on a much longer road toward institutionalizing conflict management through the procedures of a democratic state (Diamond 1995). Moreover, in some rare cases, elections can serve the aims of legitimizing the creation of new states, such as the 1993 referendum through which Eritrea was born and subsequently recognized as a sovereign state. Similarly, with the fall of Mobutu Seso Seko's Zaire in 1997 to rebel forces, one of the first promises of the new regime, led by Laurent Kabila, was a transition to democracy leading to elections in two years—an implicit, preemptive response to international pressure to legitimate his government's rule.

Elections are being routinely promoted by the international community for all these purposes, and reflected by the growing "industry" of nongovernmental organizations in the West dedicated to enhancing the capabilities of Africans to participate in them through party training and voter education. There is every expectation that the international community is dedicated to this mechanism for the long haul, and this dedication extends to promoting elections in Africa despite the disillusionment about their efficacy.

Advocating elections as an effective tool of international intervention does not mean having unrealistic expectations about what elections can and should do, or understanding that there are risks and trade-offs involved. Advocates of elections as a tool of external intervention know from bitter experience that they can backfire, that they can produce ambiguous results that fail to clarify anything, that they can result in corrupt and clientelistic (rent-seeking) behavior, or they can lead to other unintended consequences such as validating an illegitimate regime. That is, advocates of elections must be realistic that they take place in environments that are less than facilitative for liberal democratic institutions. This is especially true when the underlying tolerance necessary for managing the inherent uncertainty of elections is absent or insufficient, which is so often the case in chronically divided societies like Rwanda and Burundi. Rather than abandon elections as a tool to promote democratization and conflict management and search for some alternative, nonexistent source of stability, the international community needs to think long and hard about the policies of promoting elections. As suggested in chapter 1, the central question is not whether to promote democratization and conflict resolution, but how to do it better.

This volume, with its emphasis on electoral systems, elections and their outcomes, and lessons learned from critical test cases such as Ghana and South Africa, seeks to contribute to that debate by emphasizing the importance of, and limits to, political engineering as a means of promoting a democratization process that can simultaneously help to manage deadly political conflict. There is no assertion that getting an appropriate electoral system in place—or even getting the sequence of events in democratization or the peace process right—is a panacea for averting or managing conflict, especially ethnic conflict. Probably no amount of political engineering would ease the deep-seated, and well-founded, fears of Rwanda's ruling Tutsi minority that losing an election would not mean losing one's life. Yet clearly the structure of the rules under which elections are conducted, and the sequence of events that leads to an election, do influence how the game is played and whether the outcomes will help promote democratization and conflict management, or not.

If electoral assistance is to be provided as a tool of international intervention, how can it be better employed? The following analysis and recommendations are those culled from the participant discussion at the June 1995 United States Institute of Peace symposium on "Elections and Conflict Resolution in Africa."

### Classifying Some Problems

It is clear that many Africans and many policymakers in the international community often see elections as more problematic than helpful. Claude Ake, who describes the democratization process—seen as a competition among elites as to who will wield power—as "disempowerment," is a testament to this fact. His comment that "democracy has been reduced to the crude simplicity of multiparty elections in Africa, both by the African elite and the international community," reflects the core of the problem. Other international observers of Africa concur. Pauline Baker agrees that "without being unduly cynical but looking at the history of elections in [Africa] . . . often those who are involved see it on a much more earthy level as a vehicle to acquire power, wealth, and stakes. Any analysis that is going to affect policy has to take into account how the parties who are both managing the elections and participating in them see it themselves." What types of problems are associated with the recent spate of elections in Africa?

- Elections *can be "managed" or "crisis-ridden."* As in Kenya in 1992, where elections were used by the incumbent regime of President Daniel arap Moi to consolidate power, elections can be managed by ruling elites to provide the cover of democracy without the meaning. If they manipulate electoral rolls, districts, balloting, campaign rules, candidate selection rules, and party registration rules, and limit the ability of international players to affect the "levelness" of the playing field, they can use elections to perpetuate and legitimize illegitimate rule. When efforts to manage elections go awry, as in Nigeria's 1993 election, incumbent regimes go to the extreme of simply annulling the results, precipitating an ongoing crisis of governmental legitimacy and paving the way for a new set of conflicts to emerge. Nigeria has yet to emerge from the political trauma associated with this failed election.

"Sham" elections such as these are a problem, but so are crisis-ridden elections, in which high levels of violence, "no-go" areas for opposition or ruling parties, result in elections that are neither free nor fair. Elections that are not free and fair, or in which high levels of political violence impinge upon the outcomes, set the stage for post-election conflict when opposition parties refuse to participate and often resort to demonstrations and reprisals in order to underscore the true depth and strength of opposition to the regime. Similarly, elections can help subvert democracy if the winning party's true aims are not the promotion of pluralism and democracy, but the creation of a one-party hegemony.

• *Elections can precipitate ethnic conflict.* Multiparty elections in Africa, it has long been believed, exacerbate ethnic conflict because parties will inevitably form along ethnic lines, causing states to collapse. The "curse of tribalism" has often been the basis for adopting one-party rule throughout Africa in the post-independence period, or more recently in President Yoweri Museveni's Uganda, the basis for outlining political party-affiliated candidates altogether. That is, there is a widespread perception that elections deteriorate into an ethnic census and that ill-chosen electoral systems and political institutions exacerbate the problem of ethnic conflict.

Pauline Baker, in acknowledging this perceived problem, asserts:

> The conventional wisdom is that ethnic conflict causes state collapse. In Africa, it often happens the other way around, that once the state collapses, then you have more ethnic conflict [as a consequence of] manipulation of ethnicity by elites. If a political system is structured so that competition for wealth, status, and

> power must be along ethnic lines, because that's the only way
> you can be represented, then I think you're playing with fire.

This problem is especially acute when the electoral system chosen (or, as is often the case, inherited without change) leads to winner-take-all, majoritarian contests. Such a situation creates a zero-sum game in which one ethnic group "succeeds" at the expense of others, setting the stage for a resort to violence. Burundi's election in 1993 was one example in which the fears of a minority group (Tutsi) were heightened by the victory of a political party representing, for the most part, the aspirations of a majority group (Hutu).

- *Elections are held at the wrong moment.* The problem with zero-sum, winner-take-all elections is not one just of the electoral system, but also of the sequence of events leading to the poll and the expected consequences of the outcome. That is, at what point in a democratization or peace process should elections be appropriately sequenced? There is considerable debate about whether "early" transitional elections are best because they create a legitimate government soon, or whether the groundwork required for a successful election demands that they be deferred.

For example, the Angolan election of 1992 was not a zero sum contest *solely* because the parties opted for a highly majoritarian electoral system for the presidential election. Other aspects of the process were ill-managed—the parties had not sufficiently disarmed, the UN had deployed a woefully inadequate peacekeeping operation and election verification mission, and ongoing mediation and negotiation had failed to secure a written pre-election, power-sharing pact. Pauline Baker notes that it was this combination of factors that led to renewed violence. "This was an arrangement," she comments, "where you essentially took a one-party state, Marxist constitution, amended it so you could have an election under the auspices of the UN, and it was a winner take-all outcome."

Contrasted to South Africa, where as Vincent Maphai argues "we constituted a government before we elected it," the April 1994 election that ended apartheid was not seen in strictly zero-sum terms, and the outcome contained elements in which all parties could feel satisfied. As Mattes and Gouws point out, minority parties were able to win key regions. In addition, the parties had worked through many aspects of security throughout the course of the pre-election negotiations, such that a military challenge to the election's outcome was unlikely.

For all their problems, and despite their double-sworded nature (polarizing, yet necessary), elections in democratizing societies are an essential ingredient to the longer-term promotion of democracy and peace. In response to Claude Ake's indictment of democratization as effective disempowerment of Africa's populace, Larry Diamond argues:

> Democracy did not emerge pristine and beautiful anywhere in the world. . . . Anywhere you look you find a very nasty, utilitarian, ugly, corrupt, top-down, clientelistic process. The question is how did it get from that to a higher quality of democracy? It would not have made that progress without the operation of whatever passed for democracy itself.

> Elections are a step in the process. . . . [If] you don't start there, where do you start? What is the agenda? How do you get to the deeper democracy you want? The only way you get there is by passing through the ugly, nasty, corrupt, utilitarian, exploitative, undemocratic in many ways, civilian, multiparty electoral machine that Ake indicts, [and] that is part of the development process. You have to start somewhere. You cannot build effective states and effective governance in Africa without moving toward democracy.[2]

Harvey Glickman concurs, suggesting that the problems in elections don't mean that they will be abandoned as a demand of those excluded from power or as an interventionist tool of the international community. He comments that "We are now in an environment where you just can't postpone mass enfranchisement and elections, because it is not possible. Elections are with us as the way that democracy is seen as inaugurated, and it's the beginning of a long process." The fallacy of those who seek to abandon elections as a vehicle for achieving democratization without a concomitant exacerbation of conflict is equating the problems of *creating* democracy with the absence of democratic virtues such as quality representation, accountability, and moderation and compromise. The last, it is increasingly understood, are not necessarily prerequisites to democratization, but rather the outcomes of a difficult, perilous, and long experience (Sklar 1987).

## Critical Choices, Dilemmas, and Trade-offs

The simple fact that elections will continue to be advocated by key external powers such as the United States or the international financial institutions, as well as by grassroots democrats, the principal choices, dilemmas, and trade-offs related to their promotion deserve to be highlighted and underscored. Intervening to promote democratization and conflict management involves certain value choices; it often means taking sides in affairs that have traditionally been considered the internal affairs of sovereign states. Larry Garber comments, "It is important that we understand that we are not neutral regarding certain values, that we do have values, and that we come to the table with those values."

For example, many Westerners implicitly reject the arguments made by Uganda's President Museveni that not only can democracy be meaningfully operationalized in a one-party or a no-party state (a long-standing argument of Africa's post-independence leaders; Uganda is led by a "movement," not a party), but that a campaign without parties—only candidates—is best. Yet Uganda's no-party elections in 1996 appear to have been successful (they were declared free and fair by most observers), and they were considered a legitimate expression of public preferences.

When the international community is silent about values such as the multiparty nature of elections, it leaves those internal voices who share such values without external support. By advocating respect for human rights, freedom of association and mobilization, and, organization of interests on whatever lines (such as ethnicity), Western donors, states, and international organizations are seeking to promote specific values. Nelson Kasfir comments:

> The involvement of outsiders is never, and can never be, neutral, and it is best to recognize that and then to deal with the consequences.

> People who deal with the development process and introduction of development see that it brings new values. These values may not be in accord with what people are doing in the country which is the recipient of their attention. . . . When you are observing an election, the premise is that you are neutral. When you try to improve the election process, you're not [being] neutral. . . . You have to decide when it is appropriate to be neutral, to be the observer who is only watching and recording what is going on, and when it is better to intervene because you think you can improve the process.

Thus, recognizing that intervention involves the promotion of certain values and inherently involves certain trade-offs, the responsibility of external parties is, at a minimum, to be aware of the conundrums that inevitably occur. Surely, as the essays in this volume demonstrate, it is conceivable to create a fair and equitable electoral system in which political party affiliations are not required.

• *The dilemma of ethnic representation.* A central issue for African policymakers and for the international community is whether parties that explicitly represent identity interests, such as ethnicity, religion, region, or gender, should be discouraged or even proscribed? In recent years, several African states have turned to adopting legislation that bans parties formed on the basis of identity or religion from participating in political life. In 1993, Nigeria, for example, not only banned ethnic and religious parties but indeed mandated, by statute, a two-party system based on left- and right-leaning ideologies. Advocates of such legislation suggest that parties formed on the basis of identity are inherently destabilizing and inevitably create divisive tendencies within society.

Others suggest that no matter what the law says, where interests are real (or perceived to be real by the communities), they will find other avenues of expression that more often than not are less benign. As Pearl Robinson comments, "No matter how hard the designers of institutions work to try to restructure and shape behavior, if these are interests that people think are important, they are going to figure out how to do politics in a way that those interests get into the process." With reference to Mali in particular, she suggests that "ethnic group representation in the context of a party system that has adopted principles of power sharing and electoral politics served the broader national interests with respect to conflict resolution."

For the international community, a dilemma arises when decisions must be made whether to engage and work with exclusive, ethnic parties in an effort to induce moderation, or whether such parties should be excluded from electoral assistance programs. The more chauvinistic the party, the less likely that such an organization would be congruent with values such as tolerance, inclusivity, and diversity. Although there are no simple answers, Harvey Glickman provides a principle to guide policymakers: "[T]he task is to create a set of balanced institutions that allow for ethnic interests to be reflected and managed, rather than suppressing them or avoiding them or rationalizing politics so the ethnicity may go away."

- *Balancing multiple goals in electoral system choice.* As highlighted in chapter 1, electoral system choice has important implications for seeking to fulfill various desiderata for an election to translate the will of the people into institutionalized representation: the quality of representation (representativeness), accountability, inclusiveness/accessibility, stability of government, development of the party system, and, in settings of volatile conflict, the ability to engender reconciliation. Much of part II of this volume addresses the issues extensively with regard to Africa. A simple fact emanating from this analysis, however, supported by the scholarly literature, is that *no electoral system can promote all of these desiderata simultaneously.* There are inherent trade-offs between inclusion and accountability, for example.

Because electoral systems manage the way conflicts are organized and processed and politicized in the arena of open, competitive politics, different desiderata are important to different people. Some, such as Barkan, see representation and a constituency link (accountability) as a prime value, whereas others, such as Reynolds, see inclusion and minority group representation and influence as an overarching need. That is, depending on the value to be maximized, either a plurality or majoritarian electoral system or a proportional electoral system can maximize certain values, but this maximization will occur at the expense of other values. Electoral system choice, both for policymakers in Africa and for the international community's engagement in the processes of democratization or negotiation in which choices over electoral systems are made, cannot be treated as a decision that is simply technical.

To do so would be a mistake. As many of these essays have shown, electoral system choice has a strong bearing on processes of democratization and conflict management. Issues such as boundary delimitation, often seen as the purview of experts, are politically loaded with important implications for outcomes. One way to conceptualize the policy implications of electoral system choice is to *consider the options on a sliding scale* from the extreme plurality systems (single member district with a plurality decision rule) to highly proportional systems (such as a party list system in a single national constituency). Whether any given system is best for a society at a particular point in time is a matter of choosing among certain values.

For South Africa's founding election in April 1994, it is clear that all the parties had a common interest in choosing proportional representation (PR), a decision that was endorsed by the international community. PR played several important functions in this election, including providing incentives for intergroup moderation (Sisk 1995b). Vincent Maphai concurs, arguing that PR served to help gain representation for minorities (numerical as well as ethnic); weeded out meaningless parties with a very low threshold of representation; gave a meaningful role for minorities to play within parties—coloureds in the NP, for example, or whites in the ANC; and it helped secure the participation and cooperation of more nationalistic elements of the Zulu (through the IFP) and Afrikaner (through the FF) ethnic groups.

Arguably, in South Africa, the parties had an overarching motive toward accommodation, but the choice for a PR electoral system choice helped them institutionalize it. According to Maphai,

"The fact is that none of these parties are now in a position to espouse racial or ethnically inflammatory politics, because they are involved in [sustaining internal multiethnic coalitions]. The PR electoral system allows them to consolidate what the parties have already achieved."

When the international community intervenes to assist parties in electoral system choice—through mediating a peace settlement or expending scarce aid funds on democracy-building—it, too, should keep the inherent trade-offs among alternative electoral systems in mind. Although PR was an effective choice for South Africa, were the international community to promote its adoption in a situation such as the new Democratic Republic of the Congo, where some 300 to 400 parties exist, PR might well provide incentives for even more parties to form!

- *Trading off inclusion for accountability.* A final, related dilemma is whether parties should opt for, and whether the international community should advocate, the adoption of inclusive institutions (especially *mandated* power sharing). While power sharing may reduce the fears associated with exclusion and induce cooperation and coalition building among disputants, inclusion may well come at the expense of accountability. In Rwanda, which had a power-sharing agreement (the 1993 Arusha Agreement) before the April 1994 genocide, is inclusion of Hutu leaders associated with the mass killings really to be countenanced? This conundrum is particularly acute when extremists, especially ethnic extremists, are still armed and have the clear power to paralyze the government and society effectively. Should spoilers, or potential spoilers, be brought into the electoral process?[3]

Again, the experience of South Africa is instructive. Vincent Maphai comments with regard to the South Africa election: "The election was about the legitimization of the entire system and, of course, this legitimization would require a great measure of inclusiveness, but also to sustain that you would require the effectiveness of government. . . . because an ineffective government soon loses legitimacy." Whether elements of the ancien regime are candidates for inclusion, such as in South Africa, or simply those with the power to negate a settlement through renewed violence, such as the warlords in Liberia, the question of whether parties should adopt power sharing, and whether the international community, through its diplomacy, should encourage power-sharing pacts, will remain a question fraught with normative considerations.

### Recommendations for Policy

If elections will continue to occur in Africa, and if the international community is to remain engaged in their promotion and design, and in the actual election events, more careful consideration should be given to scholarly theory and the findings of research. The essays in this volume seek to bridge the theory-to-policy gap by providing analysis of the ways in which elections are sometimes seen in Africa and how Western scholarship offers a number of insights into understanding and improving them. This gap can not be bridged by providing blanket policy recommendations that occur to all instances, but rather by providing contingent generalizations which can serve to inform and educate those who must make policy decisions. For example, if research such as that of Mattes and Gouws seriously questions the ethnic census theory on which many choices and policy decisions are made, those making the decisions should heed these against-the-conventional wisdom findings in their efforts to promote democratization and conflict management.

Intervention is often a type of mediation in which intervenors such as the UN, regional organizations such as the Organization of African Unity (OAU), or states or coalitions of states, engage parties within a state with the purpose of affecting the social relationships among groups and individuals to promote democratization and the prevention of violent civil strife. Increasingly, and especially in the electoral sphere, it is nongovernmental organizations that engage in African states and work not only with political elites but also with mid-level elites (such as local and regional party officials) and with the grassroots (through voter education).

In proposing recommendations for these specific types of intervention, it is important to acknowledge and recognize some important facts. The first is that, as Kasfir notes above, external intervenors are not disinterested parties. All mediators intervene to promote a settlement of underlying disputes, but for different reasons and in pursuit of specific interests. It is often said that mediators have a process bias, that they are interested in "getting to yes," any yes. But international mediation is interested not only in the process of getting to yes, but also in the outcomes of such processes—the promotion of democracy, the absence of violent conflict. For this reason, mediators should be interested not only that disputants negotiate and bargain rather than turn to violence, but also that the substance of agreements they reach are desirable as well.

The second fact is that the term "mediator" in contemporary international relations is somewhat misleading. In real situations, such as mediation efforts to end a violent civil war (as in Liberia) or to avert a potential slide into violence (such as Nigeria), there is not a single mediator on the scene, but more often than not a coalition of mediators, sometimes working together and sometimes at cross-purposes. To suggest that the international community intervenes is a bit of a misnomer: the "community" is not a unitary actor and does not always operate in a cohesive or consistent manner.

With these caveats in mind, the record is clear that mediators turn to elections as a tool for promoting conflict management. Chester A. Crocker, an experienced mediator in African settings, argues:

> Elections are a subset of tools for conflict resolution. They are a procedural option, and they are an important one. They can be used to legitimize agreements that have already been reached. They can be used in cases both of a civil war and of transitional arrangements away from evil systems. They can lessen uncertainty and reinforce a win/win deal. Elections can be used to reassure people that the leap of faith they are being asked to take is not going to take them over the edge of a cliff. . . . An election is one part of a much broader package of assurances, of guarantees, and it shouldn't be looked at as an object of fear. Elections should be used tactically in a settlement context to get parties to make the really big decisions they must make.

It is appropriate, then, that the common element that is found in all the recommendations presented here are related to the process of mediation: providing information to disputants to encourage mutually beneficial solutions, pointing out the dilemmas and trade-offs and encouraging parties to make decisions with these in mind, encouraging debate, dialogue, and negotiation or bargaining as an alternative to destructive conflict and violence. Particularly on the issue of electoral system choice, as the essays in Part II suggest, scholarly expertise can help highlight the choices for those making the key decisions about how a democratic transition or peace process should proceed.

The recommendations provided here also go against the presumption that elections should be held on the basis of inherited institutions or practices. The recommendations emphasize the *choice* element: parties do have alternatives over different ways to structure, design, and manage elections, and mediators have an important, potentially critical, role in inducing parties to make choices that promote the aims of democratization and conflict management. Some choices, such as a presidential election, may highlight starkly different points of view; others, such as a PR election to a constituent assembly, may be primarily for representation and not for exclusive power. By emphasizing the choice element in elections, and ways to structure elections in a non-zero-sum manner, a premium is placed on early intervention and creating an awareness that an election can exacerbate, ameliorate, or resolve none of the issues over which the conflict is carried out. If they are to be "successful," the right choices must be made and they must be made early. External intervenors of various types can go a long way in facilitating such choices.

On the process of democratization and conflict management, mediators should consider the following recommendations:

- *Conduct specialized assessments of the cleavages in a given society, and how the introduction of democratic institutions relates to those cleavages.*[4] There is no generalizable set of rules regarding which sequence of democratization or negotiation, and which institutions, are appropriate. Should local elections come first, or should early national elections be promoted? Should parliamentary and presidential elections occur simultaneously?

As Guy Martin suggests, "Each African country faces a different situation with different ethnic, historical, social configurations. Each needs to have a system adapted to its own particular circumstances. Unfortunately, there is not enough African participation or thinking on what type of constitutional and institutional engineering should take place." For example, while it is widely believed that ethnic representation may be good for Niger (as Pearl Robinson suggests above), most scholars agree it would not be good for Nigeria. Larry Diamond also reminds us, as Glickman's conclusions suggest, that ethnicity is not the only problem. "If you set up structures to solve the ethnic problem, that may make the other problems (such as clientelism) worse." Ethnically based power-sharing institutions, he suggests, may well lead to "gravy train of rent-seeking" as political leaders engage in ethnic mobilization in order to win a place at the seat of power.

- *Take a long view.* Intervention is often faulted as a one-shot affair, in both elections that occur as transition from authoritarianism to democracy and those that emanate from protracted peace processes. As Donald Rothchild argues, "we need more attention focused on second and third elections and the maintenance process that keeps democratic systems going." There is a clear and present need to maintain the momentum created by successful elections, both in terms of longer-term capacity building and through donor assistance policies that do not leave indigenous nongovernmental organizations (NGOs) without a funding base or otherwise vulnerable once the international observers and, when deployed, peacekeepers have long since gone home or gone on to the next situation.

In addition to staying the course, a point that is increasingly appreciated by policy makers, there are important benefits to earlier intervention. Michael Meadowcroft comments, "The place where elections are stolen more than most is well before polling day, and yet the emphasis [of the international community] is on monitoring of the actual polling process. There is a very real difficulty that hordes of [observers] can come in for the actual voting, whereas all the difficulties [that have emerged] beforehand are given less attention."

Early intervention to encourage important aims such as a free and independent press, party formation and registration, voter rolls, and polling location and procedures (such as ballot design) are all critically important choices that are made earlier in the election process, as opposed to later.

• *Acknowledge and address the trade-offs and limits.* Intervenors and contestants alike need to be educated about the inherent trade-offs in various choices and the fact that intervention to promote democratization and conflict resolution occurs at the margins. Acknowledging the trade-offs is essentially a function of education: educating mediators about the choices that are available and the range of tools in their tool box (such as innovative ways to construct the electoral system that may promote intergroup accommodation in any given case) and educating contestants about the consequences of their choices and the trade-offs they are making.

Acknowledging limits is equally important. The international community's ability to affect the course of internal politics, scholars and practitioners agree, is critical but occurs only at the margins. As Joel Barkan suggests, "If the basic conditions [for free and fair elections] are not existent within the country, there is only so much you can do." Parties must be aware that the international community cannot provide the commitment necessary for democratizing or conflict-managing elections to occur; it can only strengthen and reinforce such commitment through inducements, but it cannot provide a commitment to the process when it simply does not exist.

• *Consider pre-election pacts.* Mediators should give careful thought to whether pre-election pacts, which reduce the uncertainty of the electoral contest, are appropriate in any given situation. Moreover, intervenors should give closer attention to the terms of such pacts, scrutinizing them for the likelihood of their success in ameliorating potential problems in a post-election environment. Edmond Keller argues that the international community has an important role in emphasizing adherence to the rules of the game as manifested in pacts reached among the principal contestants:

Political contestants have to agree to the rules of the game, . . . to continued compromise within the rules. The pact should be as inclusive as possible, [but] you can leave some people out [if] there are grounds for leaving them out. [The international community] needs to think about preparing the ground for these elections if we want them not to degenerate into open conflict, and do some things ahead of time, if we can, and basically engage in what people call preventive diplomacy in promoting pre-election agreements.

- *Develop a clear sense of the "comparative advantage" of various organizations and institutions and coordinate and maximize their impact with respect to any given case.* If the reality of international intervention today is a concert of actors, as opposed to a single, unitary actor, greater emphasis should be placed on achieving a more coordinated and rational strategy. Does the diplomacy of a state or a regional organization, or even the activities of an NGO, undermine the efforts of the UN? Is an NGO actually in a better situation to offer advice or guidance to a disputant than more traditional actors in international relations?

Each situation is likely to differ quite substantially on such questions, but mechanisms of coordinating intervention—such as the Burundi Policy Forum, now called the Great Lakes Forum— should be considered for replication in other situations. This forum provides a regular meeting place at which international organizations, states, and international and local nongovernmental organizations seek to coordinate their policies. That is, more effort should be made to get external parties to play from the same sheet of music. The greater the coordination, for example among state, regional and international organizations, and NGOs, the greater the influence on the parties.

- *Seek to determine whether the parties are truly committed to democratization and conflict management, as opposed to going along with the process with the hope of gaining power to the detriment of their domestic foes.* There is a critical need to be aware of the inherent bias of a mediator to get an agreement among the parties, any agreement. Thus, mediators need to help ensure that the substantive terms of the settlement are expected to be appropriate and viable. This may be indirect, such as promoting broad principles of negotiation and bargaining. Afari-Gyan, former head of the Ghanaian electoral commission (see chapter 6), argues that "If you can get the political parties in the country to agree on setting common principles [regarding electoral system choice] and issues such as how to organize parties, you already have a modicum of conflict resolution."

Yet even when parties have agreed to an electoral formula or other set of institutions, and there is every expectation that these institutions will have conflict-exacerbating rather than -ameliorating effects, mediators should not accede to the parties' choices. Mediators should not back settlements that are expected to produce zero-sum electoral contests.

• *Consider carefully the mandates for intervention, particularly with regard to international organizations.* The United Nations Electoral Assistance Division's mandate for intervention in anticipation of an election (or more broadly on a process of political reform) is inherently limited by the fact that the unit can only become involved at the request of the affected member state. However, once the United Nations is engaged, the options for achieving a viable election are multiplied because the potential for UN withdrawal gives the world body some leverage.

A request for a UN mission's withdrawal underscores that the electoral process is likely to be unfair. Particularly powerful or influential states should therefore encourage states to seek United Nations intervention when a UN presence would help to ensure a free and fair poll.

But the mandate of intervention is an important subsidiary question. Normally, UN intervention occurs in the context of an observation mission; the mission issues a post-election statement about the freeness or fairness of the poll, but does not independently verify the result. Verification missions, which are much more intrusive, have occurred in Africa (Mozambique and South Africa), but these are far fewer. Other mandate-related choices occur earlier, at the phase when decisions are made (as a result of an assessment mission) on the type of assistance to be offered.

The *type* of intervention is important, and the United Nations does have some discretion over the extent of its involvement. The United Nations, as it did in Malawi, can set conditionalities for engagement. For example, on the scheduling of the election or the creation of a representative and independent electoral commission, the United Nations could set up a situation where parties, states, and opposition movements could bargain over contentious issues on a more or less equal basis, generating more cooperative modes of working together.

A UN role is an important and symbolic one, and it therefore deserves special attention. As Robin Ludwig comments, "If the UN pulls out, it [removes] the entire credibility of the process from the international community, since you have the whole donor group and basically the entire United Nations behind the decision." In making the decisions to engage or disengage, the mandate given to observers and verification missions is critical, because at present the mandate is often too limited. Election observers find themselves in a difficult situation when they see that aspects of the election are rigged, fraudulent, or inappropriate, but the mandate limits their ablity to effect change.

With regard to electoral systems and conflict management, recommendations can also be made to help mediators.

• *Mediators should analyze the choice points, the alternatives, the trade-offs, and the potential consequences of electoral system choice.* This is especially the case in assessing the potential implications of electoral system choice for armed and destabilizing spoilers and for those parties likely or potentially able and willing to negate the outcome of a free and fair election. In this regard, mediators should carefully analyze the choices of parties and actively engage to help parties choose better systems.

When the international community throws its weight toward, or passively condones, a particular electoral system choice, it is important to emphasize that it is making a decision to back an expected outcome. For example, electoral systems (as has been shown in this volume) may be structured so as to promote the success of expected moderate candidates and parties. Yet in promoting moderates, care must be taken to find and promote the "right" moderates (those truly committed to accommodative policies) and those who can be moderate without undermining their own position.

Mediators, like contestants, should choose electoral systems that will yield specific effects. Will a referendum further polarize a divided society? Will a plurality system induce moderation? Will a PR election allow for many parties to debate a new constitution in a constituent assembly or a national conference? Will a majoritarian electoral system result in the exclusion of a particular party from representation? These are some of the questions mediators should ask.

• *Consider a wide menu of conflict-regulating institutions and practices, beyond just the nature of the election and the electoral system.* As pointed out in several chapters in this volume, the electoral system—although arguably the most manipulable institution in terms of political engineering—is but one piece of a broader institutional puzzle. Zero-sum contests are not only a matter of electoral system choice. The design of other political institutions is also of critical importance—for example, whether a presidential or parliamentary system is best or whether federalism (and what kind of federalism—ethnic or nonethnic) should be chosen (Sisk 1996). Mediators should look at the entire package of institutions with regard to their potential conflict-ameliorating effects. How will election-related disputes be managed (for example, through the judicial institutions), and what are the expected consequences of such mechanisms?

• *Seek other avenues of innovation such as the decision-rules of a parliament and incentives for intergroup bargaining.* Mass, public elections are not the only type of voting that occurs in democratic institutions. Decision-rules within parliaments and executives are also critically important and may be opportunities for innovation in electoral system design to promote more accommodative and less divisive politics. Much academic research (reflected in the list of References at the end of this volume) has been conducted on parliaments and presidencies that can be brought to bear on the myriad options for designing political institutions. Analysts often point, ironically, to Nigeria's system of presidential elections as a model for divided societies, despite that country's seemingly perpetual crisis of democratization.

Although a complicated system of voting such as the single transferable vote or alternative vote may be inappropriate for mass elections, these devices—with their arguable incentives for intergroup moderation, logrolling, and compromise—may be useful tools to promote conciliation in parliamentary decision-making rules. An important conclusion about electoral systems is that they are infinitely malleable and adaptable to a variety of situations. Moreover, the process of bargaining and negotiation itself fosters a search for innovations that are contextually appropriate for different situations.

• *Help parties help themselves by providing expertise and guidance— for example, running simulations of various potential outcomes under alternative electoral systems.* Probably the simplest and yet most important recommendation is that the international community can do a better job in providing information and comparative experience to contestants. As Larry Diamond suggests, "There is a tremendous need and scope for political and institutional learning across cases, both about techniques of electoral administration and monitoring, the effects of different electoral systems and different rules, the viability of different rules, and the comparative knowledge within Africa of these institutional choices."

There is evidence that, given current resource constraints, especially with the UN, large observer missions in Africa are a thing of the past. The trend is toward small, targeted teams in place at least three to six months before the election event to serve as the international community's eyes, ears, and hands in engaging in an electoral process. Given these constraints, it is increasingly important to consider ways in which the international community can engage, and not engage, with respect to a specific election event.

- *Consider alternative scenarios for the sequencing of elections. Sequencing is important in two respects.* First, at what point in a protracted process of democratization and conflict management should elections be held? Second, what is the sequencing of the election event itself? Are national, local, and regional elections happening at once, or are they sequenced, and if so what are the ramifications of such sequencing? There is an apparent consensus among current analysts of Africa that elections should come rather late in a democratization process, with considerable confidence-building, mass education, and opportunities for interaction and civil society building before the poll. On the other hand, many questions arise for the transitional period when opposition continues to occur outside of the political institutions; parties that boycott and violently oppose an election can spoil the entire event. Early elections, for example to a broadly representative constituent assembly, are a potential solution.

  Analysts also suggest that the staggering of elections (in academic terms, the periodicity of elections) is critical. Whether all levels of election should occur at once, whether they should be staggered, and if so in what order they should occur will surely vary from case to case. In some instances, it may be better to clarify the national situation first, in others building from the bottom up—through local or primary elections—may make sense. In each case, however, both the place of elections in the sequencing of a democratization and peace process and the stages in which such elections are being carried out will have important ramifications for the likelihood of violence.

- *Consider promoting elections as a critical turning point meant to significantly alter a situation or relationship.* Elections can be promoted as a means of ending a prolonged period of stagnation or stalemate. For several years, the international community considered whether "inducing" an election in Zaire (in practical terms, backing calls by some opposition parties) to end the crisis of legitimacy and confusion in that country's political institutions. The 1996–1997 war overtook events, but now the issue is whether to promote earlier elections in the new

Democratic Republic of Congo. According to Chester Crocker, whether in Mobutu's Zaire or elsewhere, it is like "flipping a coin." There are considerable risks. Wily incumbents could outsmart and outmaneuver adversaries and the international community, giving the regime new breathing space and precipitating further disintegration of the country.

• *Emphasize the importance of independent "agencies of restraint" such as electoral commissions and mediation and arbitration bodies.* In places where elections have been relatively successful vehicles of political change, without violence disrupting the purpose or the outcome of the poll, there have been indigenous, independent, representative, balanced, and sufficiently effective electoral commissions to manage election procedures. Such commissions are desirable for many understandable reasons, first among them guaranteeing the neutrality of the voting procedures. But they also can do many other things, such as promoting voter education, coordinating and training monitors, certifying party and candidate eligibility, and—most important for conflict management—mediating and arbitrating electoral disputes.

Commissions and agencies of this type are particularly amenable to international engagement. Such commissions lend themselves to a broader engagement by offering opportunities for technical advisers to become part of the election process or by allowing appointees of the international community to actually serve on the commission itself (as happened in South Africa).

• *Build conflict management mechanisms into each aspect of the election event.* In addition to mediation and arbitration mechanisms within an election commission, methods for handling and managing conflict should be built into other aspects of the election event. These forums were particularly effective in Ghana, as Gyimah-Boadi illustrates in chapter 6. External parties should help devise a comprehensive dispute resolution system that can be integrated into all aspects of the election process at various levels of society. Highly trained, pre-positioned individuals with conflict management skills could be distributed throughout the country—for example, as part of a monitoring or observation team—to provide early warning and engage in preventive action to ameliorate potentially violent disputes.

The involvement of conflict management NGOs in various aspects of the election event, including the often volatile election campaign rallies, can be a help in dealing with actual or potential crises that could endanger the extent to which the eventual balloting is free and fair.

- *Strengthen and systematize monitoring and observation.* Monitoring and observation of elections are a means of persuading participants to have confidence in the process, reducing some of the uncertainty of outcomes by minimizing the effects of maladministration and fraudulent behavior. Already, many international organizations and NGOs that engage in monitoring are developing an indigenous capacity to observe and monitor future elections. Although many organizations are involved in political party, candidate, and observer training, such training could be systematically improved by the inclusion of mediation and problem-solving skills in the curriculum.

However, international intervenors need to be more aware of the problem of unsustainable capacity-building, wherein the well-meaning donor community commits funds to organizations that cannot absorb the money, smothers groups with so much technical assistance that they are not able to develop their own capacity, and fails to sustain the resource flow once a critical election or transition is passed. That is, the donor community must be careful of establishing an industry to meet a short-term demand, given its track record of disengaging quickly after an election event. In sum, intervenors and donors should give attention to strategies for disengagement at the same time they are developing strategies for engagement.

### Conclusions

The Appendix to this volume shows that Africa's fifty-four states have a number of significant national elections on the horizon. These elections raise the possibility that democratization can be further enhanced, and conflict management fostered; that setbacks could occur in current transitions; or that elections could lead to new, violent conflicts. Each of these coming elections offers moments of opportunity, but also potential crises. Regardless of concerns about the meaning, timing, and ultimate utility of elections in Africa, many more will take place. Moreover, when an election fails, chances are that an entire development or economic reform program is also placed in jeopardy.

There has already been considerable learning about how to conceptualize, sequence, and conduct elections in Africa. Many analysts point to the horrible consequences of the November 1992 election in Angola as a watershed in the learning process. Chester Crocker comments, "I think we've learned a lesson in Southern Africa and elsewhere. Don't hold a bad election. Don't hold one that could make matters worse. . . . If parties appear to be moving toward majoritarian kinds of electoral systems [in situations of deep conflict], warn them they are playing with fire, and try to find ways to complicate their thinking." Without the parties' commitment to resolving disputes through democratic means, the likelihood of successful democratization conflict management is low.

The lessons of zero-sum "founding" elections in situations of high conflict are clear, at least in Southern Africa, but there are still considerable lessons to be learned. Moreover, those lessons that have been learned are not always heeded. Elections will remain a basic fact of political life in Africa. The extent to which they succeed or fail in fostering democratization and conflict management depends, in large part, on whether parties make appropriate choices about how, when, and under what conditions to turn to the ballot box. The use of electoral assistance to promote conflict management will continue to be an important way in which the broader international community can engage to help build more viable, democratic, and peaceful states in Africa for the long term.

# ■ Appendix

# AFRICA
## Basic Political Facts

Patrice K. Curtis

The economic and social development of sub-Saharan Africa is linked to its progress toward more pluralist and transparent political systems. This Appendix contains basic facts on the political development of African countries: the heads of government and how they came to power; a ranking of political freedom; and the expected year of the next national elections (see Explanatory Notes, below, for information on reading the table).

Although many African governments have conducted elections in one form or another, Freedom House, "a national organization dedicated to strengthening democratic institutions," considers only nine to be free. It considers eighteen to be partly free, and twenty-two to be not free. In seventeen countries, national elections have been held, but none is ranked as free because of continuing authoritarian features. Seven of the free countries have elected legislatures and presidents (Benin, Cape Verde, Malawi, Mali, Mauritius, Namibia, and São Tomé and Príncipe). Botswana and South Africa have presidents chosen by parliament. In thirteen countries, the current leader seized power through a coup d'état. In nine of these, the current leader was not subsequently elected nationally; these countries are ranked as partly or not free (Chad, Republic of Comoros, Congo [the Democratic Republic, formerly Zaire], Equatorial Guinea, the Gambia, Nigeria, Sierra Leone, Sudan, and Uganda). In six, national elections have been held (Cameroon, Republic of Comoros, Guinea, Kenya, Mauritania, and Niger), but none is ranked as free because of continuing authoritarian features. By 1996, another seven governments—not associated with coups—had not held national elections and also were not politically free (Angola, Burundi, Djibouti, Liberia, Rwanda, Swaziland, and Togo); however, in 1997, Liberia held national elections after a prolonged civil war and thus moved from not free to partly free. In 1995, three countries (Eritrea, Ethiopia, and Tanzania) evolved from not free to partly free, and one (Mali) from partly free to free. In 1997–1998, two countries regressed from partly free to not free: Congo-Brazzaville and Sierra Leone.

Inconsistencies may exist in the relationship between the outward manifestations of pluralism and actual political freedom. For example, Cameroon and Kenya have held multiparty presidential elections but are ranked not free. Gabon, which has had the same President since 1967—he ascended to power through constitutional succession—has never held national elections, but is still considered partly free.

*Explanatory Notes.* Last names are in upper case. "Freedom House Rating" comparatively assesses the condition of democratic freedom in each country. Freedom House develops these ratings by averaging assessed scores for political rights and civil liberties. The category "Next Election" lists the year for the next scheduled national presidential and/or assembly elections. The editors updated the table in early 1998.

| Country | Chief of State (President) Head of Government (as relevant) (All elections listed are the latest) | Freedom House Rating | Year of Next Election Scheduled |
|---|---|---|---|
| Angola | DOS SANTOS, José Eduardo. Appointed by ruling MPLA after natural death of previous president, 1979. | Not Free | None scheduled |
| Benin | AMOUSSOU, Bruno. National elections, 1995. | Free | 1999 |
| Botswana | MASIRE, Ketumile. National assembly elections, 1994. | Free | 1999 |
| Burkina Faso | COMPAORÉ, Blaise. Coup d'état, 1987. National elections (only candidate), 1991. | Partly Free | 1998 |
| Burundi | BUYOYA, Paul. Coup d'état, 1997. | Not Free | No date set |
| Cameroon | BIYA, Paul. Appointed by former president, 1982; reelected, 1992; 1997. | Not Free | 2002 |
| Cape Verde | MASCARENHAS, Antonio. National elections, 1991; reelected 1996. | Free | 2001 |
| Central African Republic | PATASSE, Félix (Ange). National elections, 1993. | Partly Free | 1998 |
| Chad | DÉBY, Col. Idriss. Coup d'état, 1990. Elected, 1996. | Not Free | 2001 |
| Republic of Comoros | ABDULKARIM, Mohamed Taki. National elections, 1996. | Partly Free | 2001 |
| Congo (Brazzaville) | NGESSOU, Dennis. Coup d'état, 1997. | Not Free | No date set |

| Country | Description | Status | Next election |
|---|---|---|---|
| Congo (formerly Zaire) | KABILA, Laurent Desiré. Victory in civil war, 1997. | Not Free | By 1999 |
| Côte d'Ivoire | BÉDIÉ, Konan. 1993 constitutional succession after death of President Houphouët-Boigney. Presidential elections, October 1995. | Not Free[a] | 2000 |
| Djibouti | HASSAN GOULED, Aptidon. Reelected, 1993. | Not Free | 1999 |
| Equatorial Guinea | O. NGUEMA M., Teodoro. Coup d'état, 1979. National elections (sole candidate), 1989, 1996. | Not Free | 2003 |
| Eritrea | ISSAIAS, Afewerki. National assembly elections, 1993, 1997. | Partly Free | 2001 |
| Ethiopia | GIDADA, Negasso. Council elections, 1995. MELES, Zenawi. Council elections, 1995. | Partly Free | 2000 |
| Gabon | BONGO, El Hadj Omar. Constitutional succession after death of previous president, 1967. National elections, 1993. | Partly Free | 1998 |
| The Gambia | JAMMEH, Yahya. Coup d'état, 1994. Elected, 1996. | Not Free | 2001 |
| Ghana | RAWLINGS, Jerry. Coup d'état, 1979. National elections, 1993, 1996. | Partly Free | 2000 |
| Guinea | CONTÉ, Lansana. Coup d'état, following death of president, 1984. National elections, 1993. | Not Free | None scheduled |
| Guinea-Bissau | VIEIRA, João Bernardo. Coup d'état, 1980. National elections, 1994. | Partly Free | 1999 |
| Kenya | MOI, Daniel T. arap. Interim succession after death of previous president, 1978. Most recent national elections, 1997. | Not Free | 2002 |
| Lesotho | LETSIE III, King. Natural succession, 1996. Mokhehle, Ntsu, Prime Minister. | Partly Free | 1999 |

| Country | | | |
|---|---|---|---|
| Liberia | TAYLOR, Charles. National elections, 1997. | Partly Free | 2002 |
| Madagascar | RATSIRAKA, Didier. National elections, 1996. | Partly Free | 2001 |
| Malawi | MULUZI, Bakili. National elections, 1994. | Free | 1999 |
| Mali | KONARÉ, Alpha O. National elections, 1992, 1997. | Free | 2002 |
| Mauritania | TAYA, Maaouya O. Sid'Ahmed. Coup d'état, 1984. National elections, 1992, 1997. | Not Free | 2004 |
| Mauritius | UTEEM, Cassam. Appointed by national assembly, 1992; national elections, 1995. | Free | 2000 |
| Mozambique | CHISSANO, Joaquim. Appointed by ruling Frelimo after death of previous president, 1986. Last national elections, 1994. | Partly Free | 1999 |
| Namibia | NUJOMA, Sam. Reelected, national elections, 1994. | Free | 1999 |
| Niger | MAÏNASSARA, Ibrahim B. Coup d'état, 1996. National elections, 1996. | Not Free[b] | 2001 |
| Nigeria | ABACHA, General Sani. Dismissed civilian caretaker, 1993. Military ousted most recent elected government in 1983. | Not Free | 1998 |
| Rwanda | BIZIMUNGU, Pasteur. Appointed by national assembly, 1994. | Not Free | By 1999 |
| São Tomé and Príncipe | TROVOADA, Miguel. National elections, 1991, reelected 1996. | Free | 2001 |
| Senegal | DIOUF, Abdou. First appointed after resignation of previous president, 1981. National elections, 1993. | Partly Free | 2000 |
| Seychelles | RENÉ, France-Albert. Appointed by SPUP, 1977. National elections, 1993. | Partly Free | 1998 |

| | | | |
|---|---|---|---|
| Sierra Leone | KABBAH, Ahmed Tejan. National elections, 1996. | Not Free (Civil war) | 2000 |
| Somalia | No functioning government. | Not Free | . |
| South Africa | MANDELA, Nelson. National elections, 1994. | Free | 1999 |
| Sudan | al-BASHIR, U. Hasan Ahmad. Coup d'état, 1993. Elected, 1996. | Not Free (Civil war) | 2001 |
| Swaziland | MSWATI III, King. Crowned, 1986. | Not Free | 1999 |
| Tanzania | MKAPA, Benjamin. National elections, 1995. | Partly Free[C] | 2000 |
| Togo | EYADÉMA, General Gnassingbé. Takeover, 1967. National election (boycotted by all major opposition parties), 1993. | Not Free | 1998 |
| Uganda | MUSEVENI, Lt. Gen. Y.K. Coup d'état, 1986. Elected in national elections, 1996. | Partly Free | 2001 |
| Zaire/Congo | KABILA, Laurent Desiré. Victory in civil war, 1997. | Not Free | By 1999 |
| Zambia | CHILUBA, Frederick. National elections, 1991, 1996. | Partly Free | 2001 |
| Zimbabwe | MUGABE, Robert G. Parliamentary appointment, 1987, when country adopted presidential-style constitution; reelected 1996. | Partly Free | 2002 |

[a] President Bédié was reelected, winning more than 96 percent of the valid votes cast. The main opposition parties boycotted the elections, however (although Bédié had one opponent), and claimed that Bédié's government manipulated election rules. Some thirty-five people were killed in violence associated with the elections, and members of Bédié's tribe who lived in opposition strongholds fled their homes after attacks by opposition supporters following the election. Bédié's party won an overwhelming majority in legislative elections held on November 26, 1995.

[b] President Ousmane, democratically elected in 1993, was overthrown and imprisoned by Maïnassara on Jan. 27, 1996. Maïnassara suspended the constitution, banned political parties, and put in place a temporary national council, with himself as head of state. He announced he would be a non-partisan candidate in national elections in July 1996, and then in May revoked the ban on political parties. The country's independent electoral commission asked that the election be postponed, but it was held nevertheless, with Maïnassara facing four opponents for the presidency, including Ousmane. During the voting, the authorities dissolved the electoral commission, appointed a new one, and placed Maïnassara's four rivals under house arrest. The new commission reported that Maïnassara won 52.2 percent of the votes.

[c] Disorganization and confusion tainted the first multiparty presidential and parliamentary elections, held on October 29, 1995. Election results were declared null and void in several areas. Elections were rescheduled and finally held successfully. Mkapa (a member of the same party as outgoing Ali Hassan Mwinyi) was declared the winner with 61.8 percent of the votes cast.

*Sources.* The majority of data for this appendix were found in the following sources: *Africa South of the Sabara 1995* (Europa 1994), *CIA World Factbook 1994, Europa World Year Book 1994* (Europa 1994), *Freedom Review* (Freedom House, January/February 1995 and 1996), and the *New York Times*, the *Washington Post*, and Reuters (various dates, 1995 and 1996). Embassies and/or consulates in Washington, D.C., also provided information.

# NOTES

## Introduction

**1.** See Howard W. French, "With a Firm Grip on Election Rules, African Leaders Rack up Big Victories," *International Herald Tribune,* October 25, 1995.

## 1. Reynolds and Sisk, *Elections and Electoral Systems*

**1.** See Rabushka and Shepsle (1972) for a theoretical treatment of this phenomenon and its implications for democratic stability in multiethnic societies.

**2.** See Sisk (1995a: 45–59).

**3.** The concept of turning points comes from the literature on negotiation. See Druckman (1986).

**4.** Remarks at the June 6, 1995, United States Institute of Peace symposium on "Elections and Conflict Resolution in Africa." Subsequent references to Rothchild in this chapter are also remarks made at the 1995 symposium.

**5.** Formulas can be either largest remainder (Hare or Droop) or highest average (D'Hondt or Sainte-Laguë) methods. The D'Hondt formula is the least proportional and often gives a slight bonus to the largest parties, Hare and Sainte-Laguë are the most proportional and lean toward favoring the smaller parties, and the results of the Droop system fall somewhere in between (see Lijphart 1995a).

**6.** In Israel, extremist religious parties are often crucial to government formation, while the collapse of Weimar Germany has often been attributed to the way in which the electoral system gave a toehold to extremist groups of both the right and the left.

**7.** Africa has experienced these problems. In the whites-only South African election of 1948 Jan Smuts's Unionist-Labour coalition won 52 percent of the vote against D.F. Malan's Nationalist-Afrikaner coalition with 42 percent. But Malan won 79 of the 150 seats and an absolute, but undeserved, majority. The new Nationalist government embarked upon the strategy of racial separation that became known as apartheid. In the Kenyan elections of 1992, President Daniel arap Moi's KANU (Kenyan African National Union) won only 36 percent of the popular vote but 53 percent of the parliamentary seats. This was because of a severely split opposition and outrageous gerrymandering of constituency boundaries to the advantage of the incumbent government—a common electoral practice in plurality single member districts that is not possible under a proportional representation electoral system. Many proponents of PR argue that the mature democracies such as the United Kingdom and the United States are strong enough to withstand such anomalies, but the fragile divided states of Africa are not.

**8.** Indeed, the only empirical case study we have of multimember district alternative voting—the elections for the Australian federal senate between 1919 and 1946—proves this to be the case. J.F.H. Wright argued that "In all ten elections with this system the results were unsatisfactory. On two occasions, parties with less than half the votes won majorities of seats, and on eight occasions, parties or coalitions with more than 40 percent of the votes won three seats or less (15 percent)." (Wright 1986: 131). The system displayed its worst anomalies in 1925 when Labour, with 45 percent of votes, failed to win a single seat, but then in 1943 Labour won all 19 seats up for election with 55 per cent of the popular vote.

**9.** For an extensive discussion of power sharing, see Sisk 1996.

**10.** Donald Rothchild has termed this form of governance "hegemonic exchange." See Rothchild 1991.


### 2. Glickman, *Ethnicity, Elections, and Constitutional Democracy*

**1.** The author gratefully acknowledges the generous support of the United States Institute of Peace and Haverford College.


### 3. Barkan, *Rethinking the Applicability of Proportional Representation*

**1.** See Barkan (1993: 85–99) and Andrew Reynolds, "Rerunning the 1994 South African and Malawi Elections," a paper presented at a symposium on Elections and Conflict Resolution in Africa, United States Institute of Peace, Washington, D.C., June 8, 1995. While considerations of ethnicity undoubtedly reinforce the high geographic concentration of the vote in many African countries, there is substantial evidence—from Kenya and elsewhere—that vote concentration occurs where ethnicity is not a factor or is held constant.

**2.** As Samuel P. Huntington (1968) wrote nearly three decades ago, the institutionalization of political practice, democratic or otherwise, requires that the practice in question (for example, the regular holding of elections, or the legislative or judicial process) be valued by both those who function within the institution in question and those who function without.

**3.** International pressure takes the form of the threat to reduce foreign aid and investment. It has been made clear to the Namibian government that to reverse any constitutional guarantees of property rights, or to transform Namibia into a one-party state, would drive away both investment and aid.

**4.** The reader should remember that these ninety-five councilmanic constituencies play no function in the present application of PR, other than to serve as counting areas for the tabulation of the national vote. Thus, although there are ninety-five such districts, the number of seats in the National Assembly is not ninety-five, but seventy-two. To avoid confusion when comparing the outcomes of PR and SMD, all comparisons are made on the basis of *percentages of seats* or hypothetical seats, and not on the actual number of seats or counting districts.

**5.** For details, see Schedule 2 of the interim Constitution of the Republic of South Africa, November 1993, and Schedule 3 of the "new" Constitution, May 7, 1996. Seats within the nine regional legislatures are also allocated on the basis of the party vote within the regions using the same formula.

**6.** Cabinet positions in the "Government of National Unity" (GNU) are allocated on the basis of one position for each twenty seats held by a political party. Although this provision was primarily intended to ensure the participation of the National Party and the Inkatha Freedom Party in the government, the National Party withdrew from the GNU following the drafting of a permanent constitution in May 1996.

**7.** *Sunday Times,* October 9, 1994 as quoted in *South Africa News Update,* vol. 3, no. 42, October 11–17, 1994.

**8.** So lacking are the requisite skills for maintaining direct contact with constituents that many MPs (both ANC and non-ANC) have sought assistance from the Khululekani Institute of Democracy (KID), an NGO whose twofold purpose is to assist legislators with their work within parliament and in their efforts to reach out to provide constituency service and maintain contact with the grassroots. Although KID is itself struggling to provide this assistance, the potential importance of the organization is underscored by the fact that it receives much of its financial support from the U.S. Agency for International Development and other donors.

**9.** Members of local government councils and regional assemblies have also departed as a result of this practice.

**10.** For example, the former regional premier of the Free State was summarily transferred to the National Council of the Provinces when he indicated that he would seek to regain his position, and a young member of parliament was named to an ambassadorial post because some party leaders wanted him out of the way.

**11.** The alternative of reserved seats for whites elected from a separate voter's roll, as occurred in Zimbabwe during the 1980s, was regarded as especially repugnant and contrary to the ANC's vision of a nonracial South Africa.

**12.** See "The Public's View of Parliament," published by the Public Opinion Service of the Institute for Democracy in South Africa (Cape Town: February 1996), and *Opinion Poll, Vol. 2,* No. 1 (Cape Town: Institute for Democracy in South Africa, September 1, 1996). In a nationwide survey conducted between September and November 1995, only a slight majority of the respondents (53 percent) approved of parliamentary performance, and a significant minority (36 percent) disapproved. By contrast, the approval rating for President Mandela was 77 percent, and only 20 percent disapproved of his performance. Most interesting from the standpoint of this discussion was the finding that while 50 percent of the respondents thought that "MPs would be helpful on matters with which they could assist," only 38 percent thought that "MPs do a good job of keeping in touch with the people."

**13.** See Schedule 3 of the "new" Constitution of the Republic of South Africa, May 7, 1996.

**14.** I wish to thank Andrew Reynolds for sharing his insights and data with me for purposes of this article. I also thank Judith Geist for sharing her data on the 1992 Kenya election.

**15.** Several methods exist for measuring the extent to which electoral formulas yield a distribution of seats for each party that diverges from its actual percentage of the vote. Following both Andrew Reynolds and Arend Lijphart, I use the least squares index developed by Michael Gallagher. For a full discussion of the various methods to calculate disproportionality, including Gallagher's, see Lijphart 1994.

**16.** The only exceptions to this rule are where support for contesting parties is dispersed as a result of some factor, such as religion or language, that divides residents of the same rural communities. The impact of caste in India, or the impact of religion in Uganda, would be two examples of this phenomenon. Conversely, the high geographic concentration of the vote in South Africa, the most industrialized country of the continent, is in large part a legacy of apartheid laws (such as the Group Areas Act), which designated where members of different races and ethnic groups could live.

**17.** See, for example, Reynolds's own calculations for the application of this option for Malawi (1995c).

#### 4. Reynolds, *Proportionality, A Rebuttal*

This chapter, which is updated from an earlier article in the *Journal of Democracy,* April 1995, is based on research supported by the National Science

Foundation of the United States (grant SBR–9321864), the Institute on Global Conflict and Cooperation, and the University of California, San Diego, and dissertation support from the United States Institute of Peace.

**1.** See Reynolds (1995c). The 4.0 figure for Namibia is slightly lower than Barkan's calculation for plurality on the basis of the ninety-five counting districts. My assessment is based on a combination of the ninety-five counting districts to provide seventy-two SMDs of roughly equal size. That calculation leaves the South West Africa People's Organisation (SWAPO) with fifty-five seats and the Democratic Turnhalle Alliance (DTA) with seventeen. (I am very grateful to Joel Barkan for sharing his counting-district data with me.)

## 5. Mozaffar, *Electoral Systems and Conflict Management*

I wish to thank the National Science Foundation and the Boston University African Studies Center for their continued research support. Earlier versions of this chapter were presented at the conference on "Comparative Democratic Elections," Kennedy School of Government, Harvard University, May 12–14, 1995, and at a United States Institute of Peace symposium on "Elections and Conflict Resolution in Africa," June 1995. The editors, Timothy D. Sisk and Andrew Reynolds, offered very useful comments that helped in the revision. My wife, Kathy, as always, was patient and offered timely encouragement, which I deeply appreciate. The final responsibility for the paper is, of course, mine.

**1.** Ake's vision also treats the masses, especially Africa's predominantly rural population, as ignorant objects of manipulation by unprincipled political elites. This treatment flies in the face of accumulated research evidence that African rural actors not only are quite aware of their interests, but respond very rationally to institutional incentives and electoral campaigns to promote and protect these interests. See, among others, Bates (1989), Barkan (1984), Hayward (1976). Both competitive elections in multiparty democracies and semicompetitive ones in single-party regimes have, of course, formed an integral feature of Africa's checkered history with democracy over the last three decades, performing a variety of functions, including elite recruitment, change in administration (for example, Mauritius), regime legitimacy, and economic policy debate. See, among others, Barkan and Okumu (1978), Chazan (1979), Collier (1982), Diamond, Linz and Lipset (1988), Hayward (1987), Hyden and Leys (1979), Mackenzie and Robinson (1960), Morgenthau (1964), Scarritt and Mozaffar (1995), Widner (1992), Wiseman (1990).

**2.** This role of elections, which fits—uneasily—with the absolutism often embedded in populist emancipatory projects, is particularly significant in transitions from autocracy to democracy. This significance is best understood when democratization is viewed not as the historically inevitable product of social structural conditions, but as the contingent, usually unintended, outcome of improvised decisions and compromises made by strategically rational actors to resolve perennial conflicts over power and resources in different historical, cultural, and economic contexts with correspondingly different institutional legacies (Bryce 1921:602–603; Dewey 1927:83–87; DiPalma 1990; Przeworski 1988, 1991; Rustow 1970).

**3.** This is the most compelling reason why arguments that democracy rooted in competitive elections creates or exacerbates social divisions and ethnic conflicts are deeply flawed. These arguments betray a gross misunderstanding of democracy as a system of governance that encourages collective decision making and conflict management. They also only embody the intellectual hubris of assuming human fallibility and the superiority of end-state planning. They are, moreover, ideologically dangerous; their proponents conveniently forget that African autocrats used these very arguments to suppress political competition and rationalize political repression. On the relationship of ethnic conflict and democratization in Africa, see Glickman (1995).

**4.** The predictive accuracy of electoral rules is an important reason for their susceptibility to political engineering (Sartori 1968). In African countries, moreover, colonial history and past electoral experiences (Collier 1982; Hayward 1987; Mackenzie and Robinson 1960), as well as the ready availability of foreign models and experts, also serve to improve the predictive ability of electoral rules. The international influence on the design of electoral systems, however, is not uniform. The advice of a German political scientist was instrumental in the design of the Senegalese two-tiered system modeled after the German system. French legal advisers influenced the adoption of two-round majority formulas in Congo and Mali, but not in other francophone countries, most of which adopted some form of PR formulas. Foreign experts were also involved, of course, in the extended debate over alternative electoral systems design in South Africa's transition to democracy (Horowitz 1991: 163–203; Lijphart 1990). On the influence of foreign models on the design of Eastern European electoral systems, see Elster (1993) and Lijphart (1992: 6).

**5.** As for predictive accuracy, alternative electoral formulas can indicate the general pattern of seat distributions, not whether seats will be allocated to individual actors. Actual allocation of seat shares depends on the interdependent electoral strategies of parties and actors, and these cannot be anticipated uniquely (Przeworksi 1991: 12). Hence, strategically rational actors do not bargain over seat shares, but over rules that will order the mutual electoral strategies that they expect will produce preferred seat allocations.

**6.** The terms anglophone, francophone, and Southern Africa are not employed here to denote the concrete historical experience or geographical location of African countries, but as analytical constructs to connote the set of contextual variables that are hypothesized to influence the choice of alternative institutional designs in Africa's emerging democracies. On the difference between denotative and connotative concepts, and the utility of the latter in comparative analysis, see Przeworksi and Teune (1971). For a similar usage in the study of African politics, see Widner (1994).

**7.** Mauritius is a slight exception in that eight of seventy seats in the country's unicameral parliament are allocated by a unique "best loser" formula, whereby, following the allocation of sixty-two seats in twenty three-member districts and one two-member district by plurality formula, eight seats are allocated to the best losers to ensure ethnic and party parity in legislative representation. This unique system was the outcome of intense independence negotiations between the country's predominant Indian population and the minority Creole and Franco-Mauritian groups. For a clear exposition of the working of the best loser formula, see Mathur (1991: 54–71). Despite its complexity, the system has worked to make Mauritius one of the most successful third world democracies in the context of deep ethnic divisions (Bowman 1992).

**8.** The exception was Zambia, where President Kaunda seriously miscalculated the extent of opposition to his regime and agreed to dismantle the single-party regime and hold elections, in which he and his dominant United National Independence Party (UNIP) were badly defeated by a hurriedly assembled opposition coalition, the Movement for Multiparty Democracy (MMD).

**9.** On Senegalese politics, see, among others, Boone (1992), Couloun (1988), Fatton (1987), Kante (1994), Villalon (1994), Wiseman (1990:165–180), and Young and Kante (1992).

**10.** The two-tiered electoral system resulting from these strategic calculations was initially comprised of sixty seats (reduced to fifty in 1993) allocated in thirty multimember districts by plurality formula, a design that clearly favored the dominant Socialist Party with its well-established organization and a strong rural base. An additional sixty seats (increased to seventy in 1993) were allocated in a single nationwide district by the largest remainder Hare quota (LR-Hare), which favored the opposition parties, since few of them, PDS (the Senegalese Democratic Party) included, possessed strong organization or established support base.

**11.** This discussion of Sierra Leone is based on information contained in an unpublished report submitted by Andrew Reynolds to the United Nations Electoral Assistance Division. I would like to thank Reynolds for providing me with a copy of the report. Responsibility for its interpretation is mine.

**12.** Other institutional dimensions of electoral systems that also affect vote-seat conversion, but are not examined in this chapter, include assembly size, ballot structure, malapportionment, and *apparentement* (interparty connected lists permitting voters to choose among competing party lists). On these, see

Lijphart (1994) and Rae (1971). This chapter also deals only with elections to lower chambers of the legislature.

**13.** For useful clarification of these differences, see Gallagher (1992), Laakso (1987), Lijphart (1986), and Lijphart and Gibberd (1977).

**14.** Vote-seat disproportionality is measured by the least-squares index (LSq index) developed by Gallagher (1991). The effective numbers of electoral and assembly parties are measured by the Laakso-Taagepera indexes (Laakso and Taagepera, 1979). The effective number of electoral parties is designated by Nv, and the effective number of assembly parties is designated by Ns. Effective threshold, the minimum percentage of votes required to win one seat, is inversely related to district magnitude: the higher the district magnitude, the lower the effective threshold. See Lijphart (1994) and Taagepera and Shugart (1989). For the Africa data reported here, the inverse correlation between effective threshold and district magnitude is r = –0.40. For details on the methodology employed to operationalize these variables for Africa, see Mozaffar (1995).

**15.** The difference between the results reported here and those reported in Reynolds (1995c) is due to my categorization of the Senegalese system as a PR system (based on the LR-Hare formula used to allocate seats in the single nationwide district) and to my treatment of the SMD plurality system governing Zimbabwe's three elections in 1985, 1990, and 1995 as one system. The unit of analysis in my study is not elections, but electoral systems as "sets of essentially unchanged rules under which one more successive elections are conducted" (Lijphart 1994: 7). Lijphart (1990, 1994) also provides the rationale for my treatment of the upper-tier PR formula as the decisive mode of seat allocation in Senegal.

**16.** Another measure of this reduction is the relative reduction of parties index (R), which is calculated by subtracting the number of assembly parties from the number of electoral parties and dividing the results by the number of electoral parties (Taagepera and Shugart 1989). For the twenty-eight African electoral systems examined here, R equals 16 percent for PR systems and 22 percent for SMD plurality systems. This reduction is particularly marked in plurality and majoritarian systems, as expected. For plurality systems, the continent-wide average number of electoral parties is Nv = 2.3, and the average number of assembly parties is Ns = 1.8. For PR systems, the corresponding figures are Nv = 3.26 and Ns = 2.78.

**17.** This approach is usefully adopted in Sisk's (1995b) study of the political negotiations leading to the choice of a new electoral system in South Africa.

**18.** Rokkan (1970: 168) made a similar point about the contemporary literature on electoral systems a quarter century ago.

**19.** Such a comparison is not far-fetched if the basic logic of comparison explicated by Przeworski and Teune (1971) is followed. This logic emphasizes comparison of functionally equivalent processes based on specified relationships of variables rather than of geographical or historical entities denoted by proper names.

**20.** This does not mean, of course, that discontent with electoral outcomes is not widespread, or immune from mobilization in support of electoral reform in established democracies. See the collection of articles in Norris (1995).

## 6. Gyimah-Boadi, *Managing Electoral Conflicts*

**1.** For a fuller discussion of the December 1996 elections, see Terrence Lyons's "Ghana's Encouraging Elections: A Major Step Forward" (Lyons 1997) and my "Ghana's Encouraging Elections: The Challenges Ahead" (Gyimah-Boadi 1997), which appeared together in *Journal of Democracy.*

**2.** For a recent account of Ghanaian political history highlighting conflicts, including electoral ones, see Boahen (1997), Chazan (1987), and, for a vivid account of the conflicts in the pre-independence elections in 1954 and 1956, Austin (1970: 200–362).

**3.** See press release titled "Preliminary Statement by the National Democratic Institute (NDI) International Observer Delegation to the December 7 Elections in Ghana," December 10, 1996 (mimeo).

**4.** I discuss the boycott of the parliamentary elections and its negative implications for democratic consolidation in "Ghana's Uncertain Political Opening" (Gyimah-Boadi 1994).

**5.** These allegations are covered in detail in the document of the New Patriotic Party, *The Stolen Verdict: Ghana's November 1992 Presidential Elections,* Accra, 1992.

**6.** The provisions establishing the electoral commission of Ghana and assigning its functions and powers are found in Chapter 7, Articles 43–54, of the *Constitution of the Republic of Ghana, 1992,* Ghana Publishing Corporation, Accra.

**7.** Only partial information on external funding of the elections is available. My own estimates suggest external funding of between $12 and $15 million for election commission activities. Some of this funding is reported in Kwasi Afiriyie Badu and John Larvie eds., *Elections in Ghana, 1996, Part 1,* The electoral commission of Ghana and Friedrich Ebert Foundation, Accra, 1996, pp. 75–76.

## 7. Mattes and Gouws, *Race, Ethnicity, and Voting Behavior*

We want to thank Anneke Greyling of the University of Stellenbosch, and Cherrel Africa and Helen Taylor of Idasa (the Institute for Democracy in South Africa), for their invaluable support and assistance.

**1.** Horowitz (1985: 97) has concluded that "census-type elections led to the decline or total breakdown of democracy in places such as Sri Lanka, Pakistan, Zimbabwe, Nigeria, Uganda, and Congo."

**2.** See Hermann Giliomee, "The National Party's Campaign For A Liberation Election," and David Welsh, "The Democratic Party," both in *Election '94 South Africa: The Campaigns, Results and Future Prospects* (Reynolds 1994); Schlemmer (1994); Johnson and Schlemmer (1996); and Giovanni Sartori, "Constitutional Court Needs Minorities to Protect Democracy," *Business Day,* August 2, 1995, p. 8. Conversations with South African politicians also reveal a surprising awareness and conversance with the idea. Members of the Democratic Party, especially, tend to cite it as a major factor in their dismal performance.

**3.** We are indebted to Andre du Toit for pointing this out.

**4.** Hermann Giliomee has argued that, "More than race, it is cultural identity—one's sense of social belonging and the values forged by one's upbringing—which in divided societies largely determines a party's policies and support it gets in elections." See "Race Still the Wild Card of Politics," *Cape Times,* May 15, 1995, p.6.

**5.** A sample of 2,517 eligible voters were interviewed in person between August 26 and September 16, 1994, in a post-election survey commissioned by the Institute for Democracy in South Africa and conducted by Market and Opinion Surveys (Ltd.). The final results were weighted to reflect an electorate estimated at 24 million voters. Only 8 percent of the interviews required substitution. Eighty-four percent of the questionnaires were completed in less than 50 minutes, and only 5 percent took more than an hour. The numbers of "don't know" or "confidential" replies were well within reason and certainly much lower than that experienced in the several years of electoral polling before the election.

**6.** We are again indebted to Andre du Toit for this point.

**7.** Our overall findings in KwaZulu, like those of many other surveys in that province over the last few years, have not matched the results of the 1994 election that gave the IFP 51 percent of the vote. While many suspected massive vote fraud in 1994, the 1996 local government election, the results of which were universally accepted, returned another IFP victory across the province, albeit with significantly reduced plurality. We believe the best explanation centers around a combination of problems in sampling deep rural areas in the province and widespread political intolerance in these areas.

### 8. Sisk, *Elections and Conflict Management*

**1.** Unless otherwise cited, all quotations in this chapter are remarks made at the June 1995 United States Institute of Peace symposium on "Elections and Conflict Resolution in Africa."

**2.** For further information, see Diamond (1995).

**3.** On the general problem of spoilers in peace processes, see Stedman (1997).

**4.** A good example of such an assessment is the one undertaken in then-Zaire in September/October 1996 by the Consortium for Elections and Political Process Strengthening, "Zaire: Joint Pre-Election Assessment Mission," conducted by the Washington-based International Republican Institute, National Democratic Institute, and International Foundation for Election Systems. This report highlighted the myriad difficulties with any election under the Mobutuist regime, a conclusion that was borne out by events in Zaire (see p. 168).

# ABBREVIATIONS

| | |
|---|---|
| ADF | Alliance of Democratic Forces |
| AFORD | Alliance for Democracy |
| ANC | African National Congress |
| CODESA | Convention for a Democratic South Africa |
| CP | Conservative Party |
| DP | Democratic Party (in South Africa) |
| DTA | Democratic Turnhalle Alliance |
| EC | Electoral Commission |
| EPs | Ethnic Parties |
| EPLF | Eritrean People's Liberation Front |
| EV | ethnic voter |
| FF | Freedom Front |
| Frelimo | Front for the Liberation of Mozambique |
| GNU | Government of National Unity |
| ID | Index of Disproportionality |
| Idasa | Institute for Democracy in South Africa |
| IDEA | Institute for Democracy and Electoral Assistance |
| IFP | Inkatha Freedom Party |
| INEC | Interim National Election Commission |
| IPAC | Inter-Party Advisory Committee |
| KANU | Kenya African National Union |
| KID | Khululekani Institute of Democracy |
| LR | largest remainder (LR-Hare, LR-Droop, formula for PR) |
| LSq index | Least-squares index |
| MMD | Movement for Multiparty Democracy |
| MPs | members of parliament |
| MPLA | Popular Movement for the Liberation of Angola |

NCD  National Commission on Democracy

NDC  National Democratic Congress

NEDEO  Network of Domestic Election Observers

NGO  nongovernmental organization

NIP  National Independence Party

NP  National Party

NPP  New Patriotic Party

OAU  Organization of African Unity

OLF  Oromo Liberation Front

PAC  Pan-Africanist Congress

PDS  Senegalese Democratic Party

PNC  People's National Convention

PNDC  Provisional National Defense Council

PR  proportional representation

PS  Socialist Party (in Senegal)

R  relative reduction of parties index

Renamo  Mozambique National Resistance

RPF  Rwandan Patriotic Front

SMD  single-member district

SPUP  Seychelles People's United Party

STV  single transferable vote

SWAPO  South West Africa People's Organisation

TPLF  Tigrayan People's Liberation Front

UDF  United Democratic Front (in Malawi and Namibia)

UNIP  United National Independence Party

UNITA  National Union for the Total Independence of Angola

# REFERENCES

Achen, Christopher. 1992. "Social Psychology, Demographic Variables and the Linear Regression: Breaking the Iron Triangle in Voter Research," *Political Behavior* 14.

Agnew, John. 1995. "Postscript: Federalism in the Post-Cold War Era." In *Federalism: The Multi-Ethnic Challenge,* edited by Graham Smith, pp. 294–302. New York: Longman.

Ake, Claude. 1991. "Rethinking African Democracy," *Journal of Democracy* 2 (1): 32–44.

Almond, Gabriel A., and Verba, Sidney. 1963. *The Civic Culture: Political Attitudes and Democracy in Five Nations.* Princeton: Princeton University Press.

Austin, Dennis. 1970. *Politics in Ghana, 1946–60.* London: Oxford University Press.

Ayoade, John A.A. 1986. "Ethnic Management in the 1979 Nigerian Constitution," *Publius* 16: 73–90.

Barkan, Joel D. 1995. "Elections in Agrarian Societies," *Journal of Democracy* 6: 106–116.

Barkan, Joel D. 1993. "Kenya: Lessons from a Flawed Election," *Journal of Democracy* 4: 85–99.

Barkan, Joel D. 1984. "Leaders, Electors, and Political Linkages," *Politics and Public Policy in Kenya and Tanzania,* edited by Joel D. Barkan, pp. 71–101. New York: Praeger.

Barkan, Joel D.; Bauer, Gretchen; and Martin, Carol Lynn. 1994. *The Consolidation of Democracy in Namibia: Assessment and Recommendations.* Burlington: USAID.

Barkan, Joel D., and Okumu, John J. 1978. "Semi-Competitive Elections, Clientelism and Political Recruitment in a No-Party System: The Kenya Experience." In *Elections Without Choice,* edited by Guy Hermet, Richard Rose, and Alain Rouquie, pp. 88–107. New York: Wiley.

Bates, Robert H. 1989. *Beyond the Miracle of the Market: The Political Economy of Agrarian Development in Kenya.* New York: Cambridge University Press.

Bauer, Gretchen. Forthcoming. "Challenges to Democratic Consolidation in Namibia." In *State, Conflict and Democracy in Africa,* edited by Richard Joseph. Boulder: Lynne Rienner.

Boahen, A. Adu. 1997. "Conflict Reoriented." In *Governance as Conflict Management: Politics and Violence in West Africa,* edited by I. William Zartman, Washington, D.C.: Brookings Institution.

Boone, Catherine. 1992. *Merchant Capital and The Roots of State Power in Senegal: 1930–1985.* New York: Cambridge University Press.

Boutros-Ghali, Boutros. 1992. *An Agenda For Peace.* New York: United Nations.

Brady, David, and Mo, Jongryn. 1992. "Electoral Systems and Institutional Choice: A Case Study of the 1988 Korea Elections," *Comparative Political Studies* 24: 405–429.

Brass, Paul R. 1991. *Ethnicity and Nationalism. Theory and Practice.* London: Sage.

Brass, Paul R., ed. 1985. *Ethnic Groups and the State.* London: Croom Helm.

Bratton, Michael. 1995. "Are Competitive Elections Enough?" *Africa Demos* 3: 7–8.

Bratton, Michael. 1992. "Zambia Starts Over," *Journal of Democracy* 3: 81–94.

Bratton, Michael, and van de Walle, Nicolas. 1994. "Neopatrimonial Regimes and Political Transitions in Africa," *World Politics* 46: 453–489.

Bratton, Michael, and van de Walle, Nicolas. 1992. "Popular Protest and Political Reform in Africa," *Comparative Politics* 24: 419–442.

Brautigam, Deborah. 1995. "The Paradoxes of Democratization in Mauritius," *Africa Demos* 3: 18–19.

Bryce, James. 1921. *Modern Democracies.* 2 volumes. London: Faber.

Butler, David. 1987. "Elections." In *The Basil Blackwell Encyclopedia of Political Institutions,* edited by Vernon Bogdanor. London: Basil Blackwell.

Campbell, Angus; Miller, Warren; Converse, Philip; and Stokes, Donald. 1960. *The American Voter.* New York: Wiley.

Carstairs, Alan. 1980. *A Short History of Electoral Systems in Western Europe.* London: Allen Unwin.

Charlton, Roger. 1993. "The Politics of Elections in Botswana," *Africa,* 63 (3): 330–369.

Chazan, Naomi. 1987. "The Anomalies of Continuity: Perspectives on Ghanaian Elections Since Independence." In *Elections in Independent Africa,* edited by Fred Hayward. Boulder: Westview.

Chazan, Naomi. 1982. "Ethnicity and Politics in Ghana," *Political Science Quarterly* 97: 461–485.

Chazan, Naomi. 1979. "African Voters at the Polls: A Reexamination of the Role of Elections in African Politics," *Journal of Commonwealth and Comparative Politics* 17: 136–158.

Chege, Michael. 1995 "Between Africa's Extremes." *Journal of Democracy* 6: 44–51.

Chikulo, Bornwell. 1996. "Parliamentary By-elections in Zambia: Implications for the 1996 Poll," *Review of African Political Economy* 23.

Clark, John F. 1997. "Introduction," "The Challenges of Political Reform in Sub-Saharan Africa: A Theoretical Overview." In *Political Reform in Francophone Africa*, edited by John F. Clark and David E. Gardinier, Boulder: Westview.

Clarke, Walter S. 1995. "The National Conference Phenomenon and the Management of Political Conflict in Sub-Saharan Africa." In *Ethnic Conflict and Democratization in Africa*, edited by Harvey Glickman. Atlanta: African Studies Association.

Coakley, John. 1992. "The Resolution of Ethnic Conflict: Towards a Typology," *International Political Science Review* 13: 343–358.

Cohen, Herman J. 1996. "Remarks," "Statement," in *Democratic Elections: Myth or Reality in Africa?* Subcommittee on Africa, Committee on International Relations, U.S. House of Representatives, April 17, 1996. Washington, D.C.: U.S. Government Printing Office, pp. 26–29, 47–51.

Collier, Ruth Berins. 1982. *Regimes in Tropical Africa*. Berkeley: University of California.

Colomer, Josep M. 1995. "Strategies and Outcomes in Eastern Europe," *Journal of Democracy* 6: 74–85.

Colomer, Josep M. 1994. "Institutional Strategies in Transitions to Democracy: The Experience of Eastern Europe," paper presented at the XVIth World Congress of the IPSA, Berlin.

Coulon, Christian. 1988. "Senegal: The Development and Fragility of a Semi-democracy." In *Democracy in Developing Countries, vol. 4: Africa*, edited by Larry Diamond, Juan Linz, and Seymour M. Lipset, pp.141–178. Boulder: Lynne Rienner.

Dahl, Robert A. 1989. *Democracy and Its Critics*. New Haven: Yale University.

Dalton, Russell. 1988. *Citizen Politics in Western Democracies: Public Opinion and Political Parties in the United States, Great Britain, West Germany and France*. Chatham: Chatham House.

Decalo, Samuel. 1997. "Benin: First of the New Democracies." In *Political Reform in Francophone Africa*, edited by John F. Clark and David Gardinier. Boulder: Westview.

Decalo, Samuel. 1992. "The Process, Prospects and Constraints of Democratization in Africa," *African Affairs* 91: 7–35.

De Nevers, Renee. 1993. "Democratization and Ethnic Conflict." In *Ethnic Conflict and International Security*, edited by Michael Brown, Princeton: Princeton University Press.

Dent, Martin. 1995. "Ethnicity and Territorial Politics in Nigeria." In *Federalism: The Multi-Ethnic Challenge*, edited by Graham Smith. New York: Longman.

Dewey, John. 1927. *The Public and Its Problems*. New York: Henry Holt.

Diamond, Larry. 1995. *Promoting Democracy in the 1990s: Actors and Instruments, Issues and Imperatives*. Washington, D.C.: Carnegie Commission on Preventing Deadly Conflict.

Diamond, Larry. 1991. "Nigeria's Search for a New Political Order," *Journal of Democracy* 2: 54–69.

Diamond, Larry. 1987. "Review Article: Ethnicity and Ethnic Conflict," *Journal of Modern African Studies* 25: 117–128.

Diamond, Larry. 1983. "Class, Ethnicity and the Democratic State: Nigeria, 1950–1966," *Comparative Studies in Society and History* 25: 457–489.

Diamond, Larry; Linz, Juan J.; and Lipset, Seymour M., eds. 1988. *Democracy in Developing Countries: vol. 2: Africa*. Boulder: Lynne Rienner.

DiPalma, Guiseppe. 1990. *To Craft Democracies: An Essay in Democratic Transition*. Berkeley: University of California.

Downs, Anthony. 1957. *An Economic Theory of Democracy*. New York: Harper and Row.

Druckman, Daniel. 1986. "Stages, Turning Points, and Crises." *Journal of Conflict Resolution* 30: 327–360.

Duverger, Maurice. 1963. *Political Parties: Their Activity and Organization in the Modern State*. New York: Wiley.

Ekeh, Peter P. 1990. "Social Anthropology and Two Contrasting Uses of Tribalism in Africa," *Comparative Studies in Society and History* 32: 660–700.

Ekeh, Peter P. 1975. "Colonialism and the Two Publics in Africa: A Theoretical Statement," *Comparative Studies in Society and History* 17: 91–112.

Eller, Jack David, and Coughlan, Reed M. 1993. "The Poverty of Primordialism: The Demystification of Ethnic Attachments," *Ethnic and Racial Studies* 16: 183–201.

Elster, Jon. 1993. "Constitution-Making in Europe: Rebuilding the Boat in an Open Sea," *Public Administration* 71:169–217.

Engholm, G.F. 1960. "African Elections in Kenya, March 1957." In *Five Elections in Africa,* edited by W.J.M. Mackenzie and Kenneth Robinson, pp. 391–461. Oxford: Clarendon.

Fatton, Jr., Robert. 1987. *The Making of a Liberal Democracy: Senegal's Passive Revolution, 1975–1985*. Boulder: Lynne Rienner.

Frost, Mervyn. 1996. "Preparing for Democracy in an Authoritarian State." In *Launching Democracy in South Africa. The First Open Election, April 1994,* edited by R.W. Johnson and Lawrence Schlemmer. New Haven: Yale University.

Gallagher, Michael. 1992. "Comparing Proportional Representation Electoral Systems: Quotas, Thresholds, Paradoxes, and Majorities," *British Journal of Political Science* 22: 469–496.

Gallagher, Michael. 1991. "Proportionality, Disproportionality, and Electoral Systems," *Electoral Studies* 10: 333–351.

Gerkie, Russell. 1993. "Kenya: Split Decision," *Africa Report,* March/April: 13–19.

Glickman, Harvey, ed. 1995. *Ethnic Conflict and Democratization in Africa.* Atlanta: ASA.

Glickman, Harvey, 1967. "Dilemmas of Political Theory in an African Context: The Ideology of Julius Nyerere." In *Boston University Papers on Africa: Transition in African Politics,* edited by J.T. Butler and A.A. Castagno, pp. 195–223. New York: Praeger.

Gurr, Ted Robert. 1993. *Minorities at Risk: A Global View of Ethnopolitical Conflict.* Washington, D.C.: United States Institute of Peace Press.

Gyimah-Boadi, Emmanuel. 1997. "Ghana's Encouraging Elections: The Challenges Ahead," *Journal of Democracy* 8 (2): 79–91.

Gyimah-Boadi, Emmanuel. 1994. "Ghana's Uncertain Political Opening," *Journal of Democracy* 5 (2): 75–86.

Gyimah-Boadi, Emmanuel, and van de Walle, Nicolas. 1996. "The Politics of Economic Renewal in Africa." In *Agenda for Africa's Economic Renewal,* edited by Benno Ndulu, Nicolas van de Walle, et al. New Brunswick, NJ: Overseas Development Council and Transaction.

Harrison, Graham. 1996. "Democracy in Mozambique: the Significance of Multi-Party Elections," *Review of African Political Economy* 23(67): 19–35.

Hayward, Fred M., ed. 1987. *Elections in Independent Africa.* Boulder: Westview.

Heilbrunn, John R. 1997. "Togo: The National Conference and Stalled Reform." In *Political Reform in Francophone Africa,* edited by John F. Clark and David E. Gardinier. Boulder: Westview.

Holm, John D. 1989. "Elections and Democracy in Botswana." In *Democracy in Botswana, Proceedings of a Symposium,* edited by John D. Holm and Patrick Molutsi. Gaberone: Macmillan Botswana.

Horowitz, Donald L. 1993. "Democracy in Divided Societies," *Journal of Democracy* 4: 18–38.

Horowitz, Donald L. 1991. *A Democratic South Africa: Constitutional Engineering in a Divided Society.* Berkeley: University of California.

Horowitz, Donald L. 1985. *Ethnic Groups in Conflict.* Berkeley: University of California.

Huber, John D., and Powell, Jr., G. Bingham. 1994. "Congruence Between Citizens and Policymakers in Two Visions of Liberal Democracy," *World Politics* 46: 291–327.

Huntington, Samuel P. 1996a. *The Clash of Civilizations and the Remaking of World Order.* New York: Simon & Schuster.

Huntington, Samuel P. 1996b. "Democracy for the Short Haul." *Journal of Democracy* 7 (2): 1–13.

Huntington, Samuel P. 1991. *The Third Wave: Democratization in the Late Twentieth Century*. Norman, OK: University of Oklahoma Press.

Huntington, Samuel P. 1968. *Political Order in Changing Societies*. New Haven: Yale University Press.

Hyden, Goran. 1981. *No Shortcuts to Progress*. Berkeley: University of California.

Hyden, Goran, and Leys, Colin. 1979. "Elections and Politics in Single-Party Systems," *British Journal of Political Science* 2: 389–420.

Ihonvbere, Julius O. 1994a. "The 'Irrelevant' State, Ethnicity, and the Quest for Nationhood in Africa," *Ethnic and Racial Studies*, 17 (1): 42–60.

Ihonvbere, Julius O. 1994b. "From Movement to Government: The Movement for Multi-Party Democracy and the Crisis of Democratic Consolidation in Zambia," *Canadian Journal of African Studies*, 29 (1): 1–25.

Johnson, R.W., and Schlemmer, Lawrence, eds. 1996. *Launching Democracy in South Africa: The First Open Election, April 1994*. New Haven, Yale University.

Johnston, Alexander. 1994. "South Africa: the Election and the Emerging Party System," *International Affairs*, 70 (4): 721–736.

Joseph, Richard. 1991. "Africa: The Rebirth of Political Freedom," *Journal of Democracy* 2: 11–24.

Kante, Babacar. 1994. "Senegal's Empty Election," *Journal of Democracy* 5: 96–108.

Karl, Terry Lynn. 1990. "Dilemmas in Democratization in Latin America," *Comparative Politics* 23: 1–21.

Karl, Terry Lynn, and Schmitter, Philippe. 1991. "Modes of Transition and Types of Democracy in Latin America, Southern and Eastern Europe," *International Social Science Journal* 128: 269–284.

Kasfir, Nelson. 1972. "Cultural Sub-Nationalism in Uganda." In *The Politics of Cultural Sub-Nationalism in Africa*, edited by Victor A. Olorunsola. Garden City: Doubleday Anchor.

Key, V.O. 1966. *The Responsible Electorate*. Cambridge: Belknap.

Laakso, Markku. 1987. "Thresholds of Proportional Representation: Reanalyzed and Extended." In *The Logic of Multiparty Systems*, edited by Manfred J. Holler, pp. 383–390. Boston: Kluwer.

Laakso, Markku, and Taagepera, Rein. 1979. "Effective Number of Parties: A Measure with Application to Western Europe," *Comparative Political Studies* 12: 3–27.

Laurent, Paul, and Paquet, Gilles. 1991. "Intercultural Relations: A Myrdal-Tocqueville-Girard Interpretive Scheme," *International Political Science Review* 12: 171–183.

Lazarfeld, Paul; Berelson, Bernard; and Gaudet, Hazel. 1948. *The People's Choice.* New York: Columbia University.

Lemarchand, René. 1992. "Africa's Troubled Transitions," *Journal of Democracy* 3: 98–109.

Lewis, W. Arthur. 1965. *Politics in West Africa,* London: Allen & Unwin.

Lijphart, Arend. 1995a. "Electoral Systems." In *The Encyclopedia of Democracy,* edited by Seymour Martin Lipset et al., pp. 412–422. Washington, D.C.: Congressional Quarterly.

Lijphart, Arend. 1995b. "Prospects for Power Sharing in the New South Africa." In *Election '94 South Africa,* edited by Andrew Reynolds. New York: St. Martin's.

Lijphart, Arend. 1994. *Electoral Systems and Party Systems: A Study of Twenty-Seven Democracies, 1945–1990.* New York: Oxford University.

Lijphart, Arend. 1992. "Democratization and Constitutional Choices in Czecho-Slovakia, Hungary, and Poland: 1989–1991," *Journal of Theoretical Politics* 4: 207–223.

Lijphart, Arend. 1991. "The Alternative Vote: A Realistic Alternative for South Africa?" *Politikon* 18: 91–101.

Lijphart, Arend. 1990. "Electoral Systems, Party Systems, and Conflict Management in Segmented Societies." In *Critical Choices for South Africa,* edited by Robert A. Schrire, pp. 2–13. Cape Town: Oxford University.

Lijphart, Arend. 1986. "Degrees of Proportional Representation." In *Electoral Laws and Their Political Consequences,* edited by Bernard Grofman and Arend Lijphart, pp. 170–179. New York: Agathon.

Lijphart, Arend, 1985. *Power Sharing in South Africa.* Berkeley: Institute of International Studies.

Lijphart, Arend. 1984. *Democracies.* New Haven: Yale University.

Lijphart, Arend. 1977. *Democracy in Plural Societies.* New Haven: Yale University.

Lijphart, Arend, and Gibberd, R. W. 1977. "Thresholds and Payoffs in List Systems of Proportional Representation," *European Journal of Political Research* 5: 219–244.

Lijphart, Arend, and Grofman, Bernard, eds. 1984. *Choosing an Electoral System: Issues and Alternatives.* New York: Praeger.

Lipset, Seymour M. 1979. *The First New Nation.* New York: Norton.

Lipset, Seymour M. 1960. *Political Man: The Social Bases of Politics.* Baltimore: The Johns Hopkins University.

Lipset, Seymour M., and Rokkan, Stein. 1967. "Cleavage Structure, Party Systems, and Voter Alignments: An Introduction." In *Party Systems and Voter Alignments: Cross-National Perspectives,* edited by Seymour M. Lipset and Stein Rokkan, pp. 1–64. New York: Free.

Longman, Timothy. 1997. "Rwanda: Democratization and Disorder: Political Transformation and Social Deterioration." In *Political Reform in Francophone Africa,* edited by John F. Clark and David E. Gardinier. Boulder: Westview.

Lyons, Terrence. 1997. "Ghana's Encouraging Elections: A Major Step Forward," *Journal of Democracy* 8 (2): 65–78.

Mackenzie, W.J.M. 1960. *Free Elections.* London: Allen & Unwin.

Mackenzie, W.J.M., and Robinson, Kenneth, eds. 1960. *Five Elections in Africa.* Oxford: Clarendon.

Magagna, Victor. 1988. "Representing Efficiency: Corporatism and Democratic Theory." *Review of Politics* 50: 420–444.

Mainwaring, Scott. 1991. "Politicians, Parties, and Electoral Systems: Brazil in Comparative Perspective," *Comparative Politics* 24: 21–43.

Malwal, Bona. 1990. "The Agony of the Sudan," *Journal of Democracy* 1: 76–86.

Mannheim, Jerol. 1982. *The Politics Within: A Primer in Political Attitudes and Behavior.* New York: Longman.

Mansfield, Edward, and Snyder, Jack. 1995. "Democratization and War," *Foreign Affairs* 74 (3): 79–97.

March, James G., and Olsen, Johan P. 1989. *Rediscovering Institutions: The Organizational Basis of Politics.* New York: Free.

Mathur, Hansraj. 1991. *Parliament in Mauritius.* Rose-Hill, Mauritius: Edition L'Ocean Indien.

Mattes, Robert. 1994. "The Road to Democracy: From 2 February 1990 to 27 April 1994." In *Election '94 South Africa,* edited by Andrew Reynolds, New York: St. Martin's.

Morgenthau, Ruth S. 1964. *Political Parties in French-Speaking West Africa.* Oxford: Clarendon.

Mozaffar, Shaheen. 1995. "The Political Origins and Consequences of Electoral Systems in Africa." Paper presented at the Conference on "Comparative Democratic Elections," Kennedy School of Government, Harvard University, May 12–14.

Munroe, Burt L. 1994. "Understanding Electoral Systems: Beyond Plurality vs. PR," *PS- Political Science and Politics* 27: 677–682.

Mundt, Robert J. 1997. "Cote d'Ivoire: Continuity and Change in a Semi-Democracy." In *Political Reform in Francophone Africa,* edited by John F. Clark and David Gardinier. Boulder: Westview.

Mutua, Makau wa. 1992. "Democracy in Africa: No Easy Walk to Freedom," *Reconstruction* 2: 39–42.

Ndulu, Benno J., and van de Walle, Nicolas. 1996. "Africa's Economic Renewal: From Consensus to Strategy." In *Agenda for Africa's Economic Renewal,* edited by Benno Ndulu, Nicolas van de Walle, et al. New Brunswick: Overseas Development Council and Transaction.

Nnoli, Okwudiba. 1980. *Ethnic Politics in Nigeria.* Enugu, Nigeria: Fourth Dimension.

Nnoma, Veronica. 1995. "Ethnic Conflict, Constitutional Engineering and Democracy in Nigeria." In *Ethnic Conflict and Democratization in Africa,* edited by Harvey Glickman. Atlanta: African Studies Association.

Norris, Pippa. 1995. "The Politics of Electoral Reform," *International Political Science Review* 16: 3–8.

O'Donnell, Guillermo, and Schmitter, Philippe. 1986. *Transitions to Democracy: Tentative Conclusions About Uncertain Democracies.* Baltimore: Johns Hopkins University.

Olorunsola, Victor A. 1986. "Questions on Constitutionalism and Democracy: Nigeria and Africa." In *Democracy and Pluralism in Africa,* edited by Dov Ronen. Boulder: Lynne Rienner.

Oquaye, Mike. 1995. "The Ghanaian Elections of 1992—A Dissenting View," *African Affairs* 94: 259–275.

Ottaway, Marina. 1995. "Democratization in Collapsed States." In *Collapsed States. The Disintegration and Restoration of Legitimate Authority,* edited by I. William Zartman. Boulder: Lynne Rienner.

Oyediran, Oyeleye, and Agbaje, Adigun. 1991. "Two Partyism and Democratic Transition in Nigeria," *Journal of Modern African Studies* 29: 213–235.

Price, J.H. 1960. "The Eastern Region of Nigeria, March 1957." In *Five Elections in Africa,* edited by W.J.M. Mackenzie and Kenneth Robinson, pp.106–167. Oxford: Clarendon.

Przeworski, Adam. 1991. *Democracy and the Market: Political and Economic Reforms in Eastern Europe and Latin America.* New York: Cambridge University.

Przeworski, Adam. 1988. "Democracy as a Contingent Outcome of Conflicts." In *Constitutionalism and Democracy,* edited by Jon Elster and Rune Slagstad, pp. 59–80. New York: Cambridge University.

Przeworksi, Adam, and Teune, Henry. 1971. *The Logic of Comparative Social Inquiry.* New York: Wiley-Interscience.

Rabushka, Alvin, and Shepsle, Kenneth. 1972. *Politics in Plural Societies: A Theory of Political Instability.* Columbus: Charles Merrill.

Rae, Douglas. 1971. *The Political Consequences of Electoral Laws.* New Haven: Yale University.

Randrianja, Solofo. 1996. "Nationalism, Ethnicity and Democracy." In *Africa Now. People, Policies, Institutions,* edited by Stephen Ellis. Portsmouth, N.H.: Heinemann.

Ravenhill, John. 1988. "Redrawing the Map of Africa." In *The Precarious Balance: State and Society in Africa,* edited by Donald Rothchild and Naomi Chazan. Boulder: Westview.

Rawls, John. 1971. *A Theory of Justice.* Cambridge: Harvard University.

Reynolds, Andrew. 1997. "The Case for Democratic Hope in Africa." In *Electoral Systems for Emerging Democracies: Experiences and Suggestions,* edited by Jorgen Elklit. Copenhagen: DANIDA.

Reynolds, Andrew. 1995a. "The Case for Proportionality," *Journal of Democracy* 6: 117–124.

Reynolds, Andrew. 1995b. "Constitutional Engineering in Southern Africa," *Journal of Democracy* 6: 86–100.

Reynolds, Andrew. 1995c. "Re-running the South African and Malawian General Elections under Alternative Electoral Systems." Paper presented to the United States Institute of Peace symposium, "Elections and Conflict Resolution in Africa." Washington, D.C., June 9.

Reynolds, Andrew, ed. 1994. *Election '94 South Africa: The Campaigns, Results and Future Prospects.* New York: St. Martin's.

Reynolds, Andrew. 1994. "The Results." In *Election '94 South Africa,* edited by Andrew Reynolds. New York: St. Martin's.

Reynolds, Andrew. 1993. *Voting for a New South Africa.* Cape Town: Maskew Miller Longman.

Robinson, Jenny. 1995. "Federalism and the Transformation of the South African State." In *Federalism: The Multi-Ethnic Challenge,* edited by Graham Smith. New York: Longman.

Robinson, Pearl. 1994. "The National Conference Phenomenon in Francophone Africa," *Comparative Studies in Society and History* 36: 575–610.

Robinson, Pearl. 1991. "Niger: Anatomy of a Neotraditional Corporatist State," *Comparative Politics* 23: 1–20.

Rock, June. 1996. "Ethiopia Elects a New Parliament," *Review of African Political Economy* 23 (67): 92–102.

Rokkan, Stein. 1970. *Citizens, Elections, and Parties.* Oslo: Universtetsforlaget.

Rose, Richard, and Urwin, Derek. 1969. "Social Cohesion, Political Parties and Strains in Regimes," *Comparative Political Studies* 7: 7–67.

Rothchild, Donald. 1991. "An Interactive Model for State-Ethnic Relations." In *Conflict Resolution in Africa,* edited by Francis Deng and I. William Zartman. Washington, D.C.: Brookings Institution.

Rothchild, Donald. 1985. "State-Ethnic Relations in Middle Africa." In *African Independence: the First Twenty-Five Years,* edited by Gwendolyn M. Carter and Patrick O'Meara. Bloomington: Indiana University.

Rothchild, Donald, and Foley, Michael. 1988. "African States and the Politics of Inclusive Coalitions." In *The Precarious Balance: State and Society in Africa,* edited by Donald Rothchild and Naomi Chazan. Boulder: Westview.

Russett, Bruce. 1993. *Grasping the Democratic Peace: Principles for a Post-Cold War World.* Princeton: Princeton University.

Rustow, Dankwart. 1970. "Transition to Democracy," *Comparative Politics,* 2: 337–363.

Sartori, Giovanni. 1994. *Comparative Constitutional Engineering: An Inquiry Into Structures, Incentives, and Outcomes.* New York: Columbia University.

Sartori, Giovanni. 1968. "Political Development and Political Engineering." In *Public Policy,* edited by John D. Montgomery and Albert O. Hirschman, 17: 261–298.

Scarritt, James, and Mozaffar, Shaheen. 1995. "Toward Sustainable Democracy in Africa: Can U.S. Policy Make a Difference." In *Post-Cold War Policy: The International Context,* edited by William Crotty, pp. 19–210. Chicago: Nelson Hall.

Schlemmer, Lawrence. 1994. "South Africa's First Open Election and the Future of Its New Democracy." In *The Bold Experiment: South Africa's New Democracy,* edited by Hermann Giliomee and Lawrence Schlemmer. Halfway House (South Africa): Southern.

Shapiro, Ian, and Jung, Courtney. 1995 "South Africa's Negotiated Transition." *Politics and Society* 23 (3): 1–19.

Sisk, Timothy D. 1996. *Power Sharing and International Mediation in Ethnic Conflicts.* Washington, D.C.: United States Institute of Peace.

Sisk, Timothy D. 1995a. *Democratization in South Africa: The Elusive Social Contract.* Princeton: Princeton University.

Sisk, Timothy D. 1995b. "Electoral System Choice in South Africa: Implications for Intergroup Moderation." *Nationalism and Ethnic Politics* 1 (2): 178–204

Sklar, Richard L. 1993. "The African Frontier for Political Science." In *Africa and the Disciplines,* edited by Robert Bates, V.Y. Mudimbe, and Jean O'Barr, pp. 83–112. Chicago: University of Chicago.

Sklar, Richard L. 1987. "Developmental Democracy." *Comparative Studies in Society and History* 32: 686–714.

Smith, Graham. 1995. "Mapping the Federal Condition: Ideology, Political Practice and Social Justice." In *Federalism: The Multi-Ethnic Challenge,* edited by Graham Smith. New York: Longman.

Stedman, Stephen John. 1997. "Spoiler Problems in Peace Processes," *International Security* 22 (2): 1–47.

Taagepera, Rein, and Shugart, Matthew S. 1989. *Seats and Votes: The Effects and Determinants of Electoral Systems.* New Haven: Yale University.

van de Walle, Nicholas. 1995. "Crisis and Opportunity in Africa," *Journal of Democracy* 6: 128–141.

Vengroff, Richard. 1994. "The Impact of the Electoral System on the Transition to Democracy in Africa: The Case of Mali," *Electoral Studies* 13:29–37.

Vengroff, Richard. 1993. "Governance and the Transition to Democracy: Political Parties and the Party System in Mali," *Journal of Modern African Studies* 31:541–562.

Vengroff, Richard, and Creevey, Lucy. 1997. "Senegal: The Evolution of a Quasi Democracy." In *Political Reform in Francophone Africa,* edited by John F. Clark and David Gardinier. Boulder: Westview.

Villalon, Leonardo A. 1994. "Democratizing a (Quasi) Democracy: The Senegalese Elections of 1993," *African Affairs,* 93: 163–193.

Welsh, David. 1996. "Ethnicity in Sub-Saharan Africa," *International Affairs* 72 (3): 477–491.

Widner, Jennifer. A. 1994. "Political Reform in Francophone and Anglophone African Countries." In *Economic Change and Political Liberalization in Sub-Saharan Africa,* edited by Jennifer A. Widner, pp. 49–79. Baltimore: Johns Hopkins University.

Widner, Jennifer A. 1992. *The Rise of the Party-State in Kenya: From 'Harambee to Nyayo!'.* Berkeley: University of California.

Widner, Jennifer A. 1991. "The 1990 Elections in Cote d'Ivoire," *Issue* 20 (1): 35–38.

Wiseman, John A. 1992. "Early Post-Redemocratization Elections in Africa," *Electoral Studies* 11 (4): 279–291.

Wiseman, John A. 1990. *Democracy in Black Africa: Survival and Renewal.* New York: Paragon House.

Wright, J.F.H. 1986. "Australian Experience with Majority-Preferential and Quota-Preferential Systems." In *Electoral Laws and Their Political Consequences,* edited by Bernard Grofman and Arend Lijphart, pp. 124–138. New York: Agathon.

Young, Crawford, and Kante, Babacar. 1992. "Governance, Democracy, and the 1988 Senegalese Elections." In *Governance and Politics in Africa,* edited by Goran Hyden and Michael Bratton, pp. 57–74. Boulder: Lynne Rienner.

Young, John. 1996. "Ethnicity and Power in Ethiopia," *Review of African Political Economy* 23 (70): 531–542.

Zartman, I. William. 1995. "Putting Things Back Together." In *Collapsed States. The Disintegration and Restoration of Legitimate Authority,* edited by I. William Zartman. Boulder: Lynne Rienner.

Zimmerman, Joseph. 1994. "Alternative Voting Systems for Representative Democracy," *PS—Political Science and Politics* 27: 674–677.

# ABOUT THE CONTRIBUTORS

## The Editors

**Timothy D. Sisk** teaches at the Graduate School of International Studies at the University of Denver. He was formerly a program officer in the Grant Program at the United States Institute of Peace. He specializes in international negotiation, mediation, and conflict resolution with an emphasis on Africa, the Middle East, and South Asia. He is the author of *Power Sharing and International Mediation in Ethnic Conflicts* (1996), *Democratization in South Africa: The Elusive Social Contract* (1995), and *Islam and Democracy: Religion, Power, and Politics in the Middle East* (1992). Sisk is a former visiting fellow of the Norwegian Nobel Institute in Oslo, and a former Fulbright scholar to South Africa. He earned a doctorate in comparative politics at George Washington University in Washington, D.C.

**Andrew Reynolds** is an assistant professor in the Department of Government and International Studies and a fellow of the Helen Kellogg Institute of International Studies and the Joan B. Kroc Institute for International Peace Studies at the University of Notre Dame. Previously a program officer at International IDEA (Institute for Democracy and Electoral Assistance) in Stockholm, Reynolds is a regular adviser to states and international organizations, such as the United Nations, on matters of electoral system design and democratization. His books include the forthcoming *Electoral Systems and Democratization in Southern Africa*, an edited volume, *Election '94 South Africa: An Analysis of the Campaigns, Results, and Future Prospects,* (1994), and *Voting for a New South Africa* (1993). Reynolds is also co-author of *The International IDEA Handbook of Electoral System Design,* published in 1997 by IDEA. He holds a Ph.D. in political science from the University of California, San Diego.

## The Chapter Authors

**Joel D. Barkan** is a professor of political science at the University of Iowa and senior fellow in the Jennings Randolph program of the United States Institute of Peace. He is the editor of *Beyond Capitalism versus Socialism in Kenya and Tanzania* (1994), a study of democratic transitions and economic reform in East Africa, and he has written extensively on African elections.

**Patrice K. Curtis** is president of Mt. Lassen Worldwide. She is a former research specialist at the Congressional Research Service of the U.S. Library of Congress. Curtis has also served as a specialist for the United States Agency for International Development, working on civil society promotion programs in post-war Bosnia.

**Harvey Glickman** is professor of political science at Haverford College in Pennsylvania, where he is director of African studies and former coordinator of peace studies for Haverford and Bryn Mawr Colleges. His books include *Ethnic Conflict and Democratization in Africa* (1995), *Political Leaders of Contemporary Africa South of the Sahara* (1992), *Toward Peace and Security in Southern Africa* (1990), and *The Crisis and Challenge of African Development* (1988). He is currently working on a study of constitutional democratization in African states.

**Amanda Gouws** holds a Ph.D. from the Department of Political Science at the University of Illinois, Urbana-Champaign. She is currently a senior lecturer in the Department of Political Studies at the University of Stellenbosch. She specializes in political behavior and has conducted research on political tolerance in South Africa. She is currently examining the linkage of political tolerance and democratic values in that country.

**Emmanuel Gyimah-Boadi** is an assistant professor in the School of International Service at American University in Washington, D.C. A graduate of the doctoral program in political science at the University of California, Davis, Gyimah-Boadi has taught at the University of Ghana, the University of Swaziland, and the Nitze School of Advanced International Studies in Washington. He is the editor of *Ghana Under PNDC Rule* (Codesria, London, 1993), and the author of numerous articles on African politics. He is currently working under a grant from the United States Institute of Peace on democratization as conflict resolution in Africa.

**Robert B. Mattes** holds a Ph.D. from the Department of Political Science at the University of Illinois, Urbana-Champaign. He has conducted research in both the United States and South Africa on the political impact of public opinion polling. In 1994, he served as a political analyst with South Africa's Independent Electoral Commission. Since 1995, he has been manager of the Public Opinion Service of the Institute for Democracy in South Africa (Idasa).

Over the last two years, he has been examining the impact of race, ethnicity, and identity on voting behavior and democratic values in South Africa.

**Shaheen Mozaffar** is associate professor of political science at Bridgewater State College and research fellow of the Boston University African Studies Center. He is the author of articles and book chapters on the colonial state, ethnic politics, and democratization in Africa. He was a Fulbright lecturer in Nigeria and has also conducted research in Ghana. He has been a consultant to the U.S. Agency for International Development's Africa Bureau, division of democracy and governance, and has most recently served as a consultant to the Fiji Constitution Review Commission under the auspices of the United Nations Electoral Assistance Division. He is currently engaged in a comparative study of constitutional design and electoral systems in Africa's emerging democracies.

# PARTICIPANTS IN THE SYMPOSIUM

| | |
|---|---|
| Dr. K. Afari-Gyan | Chairman, Electoral Commission of Ghana |
| Dr. Claude Ake (deceased) | Center for Advanced Social Science |
| Dr. Pauline Baker | Fund for Peace |
| Dr. Joel Barkan | Department of Political Science, University of Iowa |
| Mr. Joe C. Baxter | International Foundation for Electoral Systems |
| Ms. Melanie Bixby | Bureau of African Affairs, U.S. Department of State |
| Dr. Chester Crocker | United States Institute of Peace |
| Ms. Patrice Curtis | Library of Congress |
| Ms. Vivian Lowery Derryck | Formerly of the African-American Institute |
| Dr. Larry Diamond | Hoover Institution, Stanford University |
| Mr. Larry Garber | U.S. Agency for International Development |
| Dr. Harvey Glickman | Department of Political Science, Haverford College |
| Dr. Amanda Gouws | Department of Political Science, University of Stellenbosch |
| Dr. Harriet Hentges | United States Institute of Peace |
| Dr. Nelson Kasfir | Department of Government, Dartmouth College |
| Dr. Edmond Keller | African Studies Center, University of California, Los Angeles |
| Mr. Will Kennedy | Electoral Assistance Division, United Nations |
| Mr. Keith Klein | International Foundation for Electoral Systems |
| Dr. Robin Ludwig | Electoral Assistance Division, United Nations |
| Dr. Vincent Maphai | Human Sciences Research Council, South Africa |

| | |
|---|---|
| Dr. Guy Martin | Department of Political Science, Clark Atlanta University |
| Dr. Robert Mattes | Institute for Democracy in South Africa |
| Mr. Steven McDonald | Formerly with the African-American Institute |
| Ms. Gay McDougall | International Human Rights Law Group |
| Mr. Ned McMahon | National Democratic Institute for International Affairs |
| Mr. Michael Meadowcroft | Electoral Reform Society (UK) |
| Dr. Shaheen Mozaffar | Bridgewater State College |
| Dr. Andrew Reynolds | Department of Government, University of Notre Dame |
| Mr. Rob Richie | Center for Voting and Democracy |
| Dr. Pearl Robinson | International Relations Department, Tufts University |
| Dr. Donald S. Rothchild | Department of Political Science, University of California, Davis |
| Dr. Timothy Sisk | Graduate School of International Studies, University of Denver |
| Dr. David R. Smock | United States Institute of Peace |
| Mr. Edward Stewart | International Republican Institute |
| Dr. Astri Suhrke | Christian Michelsen Institute, Norway |
| Mr. Stephen Weissman | |
| Dr. Ernest Wilson | Center for Strategic and International Studies |
| Dr. Howard Wolpe | U.S. Special Envoy for Burundi |
| Ms. Amy Young | U.S. Agency for International Development |

# INDEX

# Elections and Conflict Management in Africa

This book is set in Garamond, and the display type is Bodega Sans. Marie Marr designed the book's cover and Day Dosch and Joan Engelhardt designed the interior. Day Dosch did the page makeup. Cynthia Benjamins edited the book.